HEADS UP
SOCIOLOGY

Senior Editor Scarlett O'Hara
Senior Designer Sheila Collins
Editor Ann Baggaley
Designers Mik Gates, Kit Lane
Illustration Sheila Collins, Mik Gates,
Kit Lane, Gus Scott
US Editors Margaret Parrish, Christy Lusiak

Managing Editor Francesca Baines
Managing Art Editor Phil Letsu
Publisher Andrew Macintyre
Publishing Director Jonathan Metcalf
Associate Publishing Director Liz Wheeler
Art Director Karen Self
Pre-Production Producer Jacqueline Street
Senior Producer Gary Batchelor
Senior Jacket Designer Mark Cavanagh
Jacket Designer Suhita Dharamjit
Jacket Design Development Manager Sophia MTT
Senior DTP Designer Harish Aggarwal
Jackets Editorial Coordinator Priyanka Sharma
Jacket Editor Claire Gell

First American Edition, 2018
Published in the United States by DK Publishing
345 Hudson Street, New York, New York 10014

A WORLD OF IDEAS:
SEE ALL THERE IS TO KNOW
www.dk.com

HEADS UP
SOCIOLOGY

WRITTEN BY
DR. CHRIS YUILL AND
DR. CHRISTOPHER THORPE

CONSULTANT
DR. MEGAN TODD

Contents

06 What is SOCIOLOGY?

08 What do SOCIOLOGISTS DO?

10 RESEARCH methods

Who AM I?

14 What is my IDENTITY?

16 GIRLS and BOYS

18 WOMEN and work

20 Biography:
JUDITH BUTLER

22 What's my TRIBE?

24 Does RACE matter?

26 Biography:
ELIJAH ANDERSON

28 Who do you LOVE?

30 AGE and society

32 What does FAMILY mean?

34 Are we all MIDDLE
CLASS now?

36 Biography:
KARL MARX

38 Identity: IN CONTEXT

Does society EXIST?

42 What do schools TEACH?

44 Are INSTITUTIONS a
good thing?

46 Biography:
CHARLES WRIGHT MILLS

48 Who holds the POWER?

50 What role does RELIGION
play in society?

52 Does RELIGION still
MATTER?

54 RURAL life versus
URBAN life

56 A sense of COMMUNITY

58 Biography:
MAX WEBER

60 WHY do we WORK?

62 How is work CHANGING?

64 Biography:
ARLIE R. HOCHSCHILD

66 WATCHING the workers

68 Social institutions:
IN CONTEXT

When it all goes WRONG

72 Why do people commit CRIMES?

74 Biography:
ÉMILE DURKHEIM

76 BREAKING society's RULES

78 White-collar CRIME

80 Are we all on CAMERA?

82 WHODUNNIT?

84 Biography:
HOWARD BECKER

86 HEALTH and equality

88 Not FITTING in

90 Crime and health:
IN CONTEXT

Why is the world so UNFAIR?

94 SuperRICH!

96 Wealth and STATUS

98 The POVERTY trap

100 Who's to BLAME?

102 Where did RACISM come from?

104 Why haven't developing countries DEVELOPED yet?

106 Biography:
BOAVENTURA
DE SOUSA SANTOS

108 Is GLOBALIZATION a good thing?

110 GLOCALIZATION

112 Biography:
SASKIA SASSEN

114 What's our IMPACT on the PLANET?

116 Biography:
ANTHONY GIDDENS

118 Wealth and development:
IN CONTEXT

Modern CULTURE

122 I SHOP therefore I am?

124 What is CULTURE?

126 Biography:
PIERRE BOURDIEU

128 LEISURE time

130 We are living in UNCERTAIN times

132 Biography:
ZYGMUNT BAUMAN

134 Does the MASS MEDIA affect YOU?

136 Who owns the MEDIA?

138 Who DECIDES what's news?

140 Where do you get your NEWS from?

142 What does the INTERNET DO for us?

144 Do you live ONLINE?

146 Culture and the media:
IN CONTEXT

148 Directory of sociologists

152 Glossary

156 Index and acknowledgments

What is **SOCIOLOGY**?

ARE MEN AND WOMEN REALLY THAT DIFFERENT? WHY ARE SOME PEOPLE SUPERRICH WHEN OTHERS ARE HOMELESS? WHY DO SOME PEOPLE COMMIT CRIMES? THESE ARE SOME OF THE QUESTIONS AT THE HEART OF LIFE AS A HUMAN BEING, AND IF YOU HAVE ASKED QUESTIONS LIKE THESE, THEN YOU ARE ALREADY A BUDDING SOCIOLOGIST. SOCIOLOGY IS THE STUDY OF SOCIETY, BUT IT IS ALSO A FRESH WAY OF THINKING ABOUT THE WORLD.

Sociologists, the people who study sociology, are interested in the ways in which individuals, groups, and societies are shaped and how they interact with one other. They look at how social institutions such as the family, the education system, religions, and governments work, and consider the ways in which the institutions impact people's lives.

The branch of social sciences known as sociology emerged at the end of the 18th century, when much of the world was changing rapidly because of increasing industrialization. German philosopher Karl Marx, and other thinkers of the time, were concerned with growing social inequality. They wanted to understand what was happening and the effect it was having on people and societies. Sociology is a social science that uses a range of methods to investigate

the social world. Using evidence and logic, it develops and tests theories such as Marxism and feminism, which can help this process. To be a sociologist also requires what US sociologist Charles Wright Mills called the "Sociological Imagination"—the ability to challenge common sense ideas about the world and to ask new questions. For instance, we might ask "Why do we have problems like racism and homophobia?" or "Is the news truthful?"

Most importantly, sociology offers the possibility of understanding our lives more fully and of making them better. As Polish sociologist Zygmunt Bauman said, the purpose of sociology is "to come to the help of the individual."

What do SOCIOLOGISTS DO?

ACADEMIC SOCIOLOGISTS

Professor

A professor works in a college or university. He or she gives lectures to large groups of students in a particular area of sociology and discusses it with them in small groups or seminars. A professor also writes books and articles (papers) about sociology.

Researcher

Also working in a college or university, a researcher spends his or her time looking into projects that will reveal more about important social issues.

SOCIOLOGISTS IN PUBLIC SERVICE

Police

A lot of sociology is about why things go wrong for some individuals. This knowledge can be useful for people working in the police or prison systems. It can help them understand why people break the law and how they can be helped.

Social worker

Sociology highlights why some people struggle in society. Understanding the issues people face and how these issues affect them can help a social worker improve the lives of vulnerable or socially excluded people (people who feel isolated or neglected in society).

SOCIOLOGISTS IN BUSINESS

Recruitment

Understanding what motivates people and the opportunities that are available to them in society can help anyone who works in recruitment to match the right person to the right job.

SOCIOLOGY IS CONCERNED WITH PEOPLE, AND SOCIOLOGISTS LEARN A VARIETY OF SKILLS THAT CAN BE USED IN MANY DIFFERENT OCCUPATIONS. SOCIOLOGISTS ARE ABLE TO ANALYZE INFORMATION, THEY HAVE INQUIRING MINDS, AND THEY LIKE TO DIG DEEPER INTO SOCIETAL ISSUES THAN MOST PEOPLE. MANY SOCIOLOGISTS WILL WANT TO BRING THEIR SKILLS AND KNOWLEDGE TO AREAS OF WORK THAT HELP THOSE WHO ARE STRUGGLING IN SOCIETY, OR THEY MAY ENJOY WORKING TO BRING OUT THE BEST IN OTHERS.

Some academic sociologists spend most of their time writing books and papers for publication in journals. The books may serve to introduce readers to the subject or be in-depth discussions and analyses of a particular topic.

Writer

Sociology helps people understand how society works and what makes a good society, which is something every politician should know. Sociology can uncover causes of inequality and discrimination.

Politician

A policy analyst works to think up government policies that will help society run more smoothly and fairly for everyone.

Policy analyst

Studying sociology can help uncover what motivates and stimulates people—ideal skills for a teacher. Knowing the issues that some families face in society also helps teachers find ways to work with students who are struggling.

Teacher

Working in human resources (HR) in an office or other workplace requires working with people to develop their potential. Sociology can help explain how and why people behave in certain ways in an environment such as an office.

Human resources

Understanding how society works and noticing people's patterns of behavior are ideal skills for working in marketing. This knowledge can help marketing professionals develop a marketing strategy for a product.

Marketing

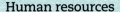

Research **METHODS**

SOCIOLOGY IS A SCIENCE—OR RATHER A SOCIAL SCIENCE—THAT SEEKS TO FIND
OUT HOW SOCIETY WORKS. LIKE OTHER SCIENCE SUBJECTS, IT RELIES ON RESEARCH
TO MAKE NEW DISCOVERIES AND GAIN INSIGHT. SOCIOLOGISTS DO NOT CONDUCT
EXPERIMENTS IN THE LABORATORY; THEY TRY TO ENGAGE AS MUCH AS POSSIBLE
WITH PEOPLE TO FIND OUT HOW THEY UNDERSTAND THE SOCIETY IN WHICH THEY LIVE.
THESE ARE SOME OF THE MOST COMMON WAYS A SOCIOLOGIST GATHERS INFORMATION.

Interviews

An approach called a "semi-structured
interview," is a sort of guided conversation.
The interviewer creates a relaxed atmosphere
for the participants to talk freely about how
the subject being researched affects their
lives. It does not matter whether something
is true or false. What matters is what is
meaningful for the people being interviewed,
and how they interpret and understand the
world around them.

Focus groups

Setting up a focus group is a way to find
out how a small group of people feel about
a particular situation. The sociologist gathers
between six and 12 people who typically
all have something in common. For example,
they could all be members of the same
community, workplace, or youth group. As well
as gathering information about the subject of
the research, the sociologist is also observing
how the members of the group interact.

Surveys and statistics

If a researcher wants to gain information from a larger number of participants, he or she may use a survey. This consists of carefully planned questions that have a limited number of responses. The researcher will analyze the results and identify patterns.

Statistics from governments or organizations (called data sets) provide information based on the responses of thousands of people. "Big data" gathered from huge amounts of people and processed by computers, brings insights into the attitudes of people around the world.

Ethnography

In some cases, a researcher tries to blend in with a group, such as a community or a workplace, spending a long time, possibly years, observing and noting how the members of the group live and what their values and customs are. The goal of this process, known as ethnography, is to get as close to the experience of the members as possible. It can be a challenging undertaking; to be part of a community and not reveal that you are a researcher requires a lot of planning, although you can also take a more open approach.

Who **AM I?**

What is my identity?

GIRLS and BOYS

WOMEN and work

What's my TRIBE?

Does RACE matter?

WHO do you LOVE?

AGE and SOCIETY

What does FAMILY mean?

Are we all MIDDLE CLASS now?

Our identity is influenced by factors such as our class, ethnicity, age, and gender as well as our tastes in things such as fashion and music. The process of finding out who we are and where we belong takes place within society. Sociologists explore the relationship between individuals and the society they live in.

What is my

WHERE DOES OUR IDENTITY COME FROM? SOCIOLOGISTS DO NOT SEE OUR IDENTITY AS A FIXED THING THAT WE ARE BORN WITH, BUT AS A MIXTURE OF THINGS, SOME OF WHICH WE CANNOT CHANGE EASILY, SUCH AS OUR RACE AND GENDER, AND OTHERS THAT WE CAN, SUCH AS OUR JOBS OR THE WAY WE DRESS.

A changing world

In previous generations, many people had one job for their whole lives and this gave them a sense of security and certainty about who they were. There were also powerful institutions that were deeply embedded in people's lives, such as religion, which also provided people with a strong sense of how they fit into the world. Today, however, these factors are less fixed in people's lives and these certainties no longer exist.

Factors that create identity

Sociologists study how identity, the sense of who one is, emerges out of a relationship between the individual and various parts and processes of society. British sociologist Richard Jenkins has spent time thinking about how identity is formed. He describes it as a "dialectical" process with society. What he means by dialectical in this case is that two opposing aspects of identity come together to create something new. The two aspects are personal characteristics, over which the individual may be able to exert some control, and social characteristics including class, gender, sexuality, and ethnicity, over which people have considerably less control.

The various social characteristics of identity are discussed in greater depth later in this chapter, where we discover that they are "social constructions,"

> The first "selfie" was taken by Robert Cornelius, in Philadelphia in 1839.

IDENTITY?

BE YOURSELF; EVERYONE ELSE IS ALREADY TAKEN.

OSCAR WiLDE, 19TH-CENTURY iRiSH PLAYWRiGHT

See also: 122–123, 144–145

meaning that something that may seem "natural" is actually the outcome of social, historical, and cultural developments that have changed over time. This is, in many respects, the key to understanding what sociology is about—it explores how so much of what happens around and to people can be explained by understanding the society in which the person exists.

Managing identity

For some people, maintaining their identity can be difficult. They can have a lifestyle or perhaps an illness that leads them, in particular circumstances, to be unfairly stigmatized (or marked as being different or bad). US sociologist Erving Goffman in his book *Stigma* (1963) analyzed the effect that being stigmatized can have on someone. He talks about how some people are required to manage their identity to avoid negative reactions, such as people who are gay, have been in prison, or have suffered from mental illness. Having to do this requires exhaustive planning and causes psychological stress so as not to reveal a secret accidently.

In the 1990s, British sociologist Anthony Giddens tried to work out which aspects of our identity are constant, when so many traditions have changed. He says that people increasingly turn to their bodies as something they can control, and it becomes the area where people display their identity. Think about how many "selfies" are posted on social media, and how much time and money people spend on their appearance. People often express who they would like to be by how they present their bodies, such as by getting a tattoo as a way to show which social group they belong to.

So finding your identity is an important process that takes place within your society.

SOCIAL CHARACTERISTICS

PERSONAL CHARACTERISTICS

CAN YOU CHOOSE WHO YOU WANT TO BE?

We are all different

Our identity comes from a mixture of factors, some of which are fixed, and others that we can choose. We do not exist in isolation, and the society we live in also helps to create our identity.

GIRLS and BOYS

WE MAY THINK WE KNOW WHAT IT MEANS TO BE A BOY OR A GIRL—IT SEEMS LIKE SOMETHING COMPLETELY NATURAL. WE ARE BORN AS EITHER A BOY OR A GIRL AND HOW WE BEHAVE REFLECTS THIS BIOLOGICAL FACT. HOWEVER, SOCIOLOGY TELLS US THAT WHAT MAKES UP GENDER MAY HAVE A LOT TO DO WITH THE SOCIETY IN WHICH WE LIVE.

The UK's *Telegraph* newspaper listed 25 English words that are used to describe women (and not men), including "airhead," "bossy," and "sassy."

Is it all about biology?

Is our gender identity (whether we are a boy or a girl) linked only to our biology, or is it more complex than that? What constructs our gender has a great deal to do with the society and times in which we live. If something is natural or genetic, then it would be the same in every place and in every historical period. What we find though, is that what it means to be male or female changes constantly: it is never a fixed thing.

For example, what it was to be a man or woman a hundred years ago is quite different from what it is to be a woman or man today. A hundred years ago, women were not allowed to vote and were often discouraged from offering opinions; now a woman can run for president of the United States. There are all types of associations with gender that have also changed. The color pink is now strongly linked with young girls, with clothes and toys for little girls all coming in a very similar shade. In Victorian England, however, pink was a boy's color—it was seen as a "younger" form of the "manly" color red.

Being socialized

Sociologists have identified a process, called socialization as the way in which we learn how to fit into our society by finding out what is acceptable and what is expected of us. Gender socialization

GIRLS LEARN HOW TO BE GIRLS FROM THE SOCIETY THEY GROW UP IN...

refers to a range of obvious and subtle processes that shape our behavior as girls or boys. US sociologist Iris Marion Young's book, *Throwing Like a Girl*, explores how boys and girls are socialized to behave differently. For example, girls may be encouraged to think that they cannot throw a ball well and that their bodies are fragile and weak, while boys are often encouraged to think the opposite.

Putting on a performance

Another way of thinking about how our gender is constructed by society is provided by US sociologist Judith Butler. She believes that we learn to act as male or female. It is the impersonation of socially expected behavior (what she refers to as "gender performativity") that constructs gender. Gender is therefore something that is external rather than internal to us. This constant performing of gender creates a false impression that what is a social practice is just a natural expression of a person's sex.

Australian sociologist Raewyn Connell shares Butler's perspective that gender is a social construct. In her analysis, she claims that gender is arranged in a hierarchy, with masculinity valued higher than femininity. She believes there are different ways to be a man or a woman, and these behaviors, which she calls "masculinities" and

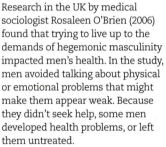

I DON'T NEED HELP

Research in the UK by medical sociologist Rosaleen O'Brien (2006) found that trying to live up to the demands of hegemonic masculinity impacted men's health. In the study, men avoided talking about physical or emotional problems that might make them appear weak. Because they didn't seek help, some men developed health problems, or left them untreated.

"femininities," are graded in society, with some regarded as more masculine or feminine than others. The most powerful form of masculinity is "hegemonic masculinity." Hegemonic refers to an idea or group of people that are dominant in a society. This type of masculinity is a style that is tough, successful, outgoing, and "macho." For Connell, however, it is the behavior that is crucial, not the biological sex. So, women can also embody hegemonic masculinity. For example, German chancellor Angela Merkel and former British prime minister Margaret Thatcher could be said to possess the traits associated with hegemonic masculinity.

Gender, then, is a state of being that is explained not by thinking in terms of biology, but by referring to wider society and its expectations of what it means to be a man or a woman.

...AND THAT'S HOW BOYS LEARN TO BE BOYS, TOO.

⮌ Learning to fit in

The process of socialization means that boys and girls learn what sort of behavior is acceptable in society and what is not. If boys want to play with dolls they may be discouraged in order to fit in with what's considered "normal."

It will be around 2150 before the gender pay gap closes in the US and, possibly, 2070 in the UK.

WOMEN

MANY SOCIETIES DISCRIMINATE AGAINST WOMEN SO THAT THEY HAVE FEWER OPPORTUNITIES AND EARN LESS THAN MEN. ALTHOUGH FOR MOST WOMEN, "WORK" IS MORE THAN THEIR PAID EMPLOYMENT—THEY OFTEN WORK IN THE HOME OR CARE FOR OTHERS, AND THIS WORK IS USUALLY UNPAID.

Jobs for women

To fill a pressing shortage of factory workers during World War II, the US government began a campaign to recruit more women workers (see box below). The government was trying to reverse the dominant gender stereotype that dictated that women were not able to work in factories, and were better suited to being secretaries or housewives. The campaign was effective and the workforce swelled by a great many extra women. After the war finished, however, the men returned and the need for women workers was reduced. Now all the women who had been recruited lost their jobs, and the prewar stereotype of the jobs women could do was quickly reinstated.

This example illustrates how women's work is determined by the kind of society in which they live. Clearly during World War II women were capable of doing the same work as men, once they were allowed to, but discrimination in society has meant that they are not always given the same opportunities as men.

A WOMAN'S WORK IS NEVER DONE.

ANONYMOUS

While women achieve the same educational levels as men, many societies discriminate against them, holding them in a lower position than men, so that when it comes to access to employment, many restrictions are placed on women.

The glass ceiling

Trapped between a glass ceiling and a sticky floor is one way of summarizing women's experiences of work. The glass ceiling refers to women being able to see the top jobs in the company in which they work but not being able to break through and gain those positions. The sticky floor refers to the trap for women of low-paid, low-status, and low-skilled jobs such as waitressing or cleaning.

Despite the decades of feminism (a political and social movement that campaigns for equality between men and women) and equal pay legislation in Europe and North America, a woman's weekly wage is significantly less than that of a man in many countries. In the US, the gender pay gap—the difference between men's and women's pay—is 20%, while in the UK the same gap is just under 14%. Another way of expressing this UK figure is to imagine that if men's pay lasted for 12 months from January 1st, women's would last only until the October 19th—for the rest of the year women are effectively working unpaid.

ROSIE THE RIVETER

During World War II, the US government invented a character named Rosie the Riveter to encourage women to work in factories. Rosie appeared on posters wearing the blue coveralls usually worn by men. She appeared with the slogan "We Can Do It" to inspire women to take up the challenge.

and work

Housework

For many women "work" consists of more than paid employment; it frequently includes caring for children as well as household chores. Published in the mid-1970s, British sociologist Ann Oakley's book *The Sociology of Housework* highlighted how domestic work is just as important, demanding, and valuable as paid work. Although Oakley's book was written 40 years ago, the point it makes is still relevant. Women still do more housework and childcare than men.

Research in Britain in 2011 by Man Yee Kan and colleagues found that on average men do 148 minutes of chores around the house per week while women do 280 minutes. This situation affects men as well as women, since both are limited by gender stereotypes, or fixed ideas about what jobs men and women can do.

The inequalities that exist in the workplace reflect other inequalities that women face in society. The problems women face at work are another example of discrimination against women.

See also: 48–49, 64–65

☉ Women's roles

There are still fewer women in top executive positions in business, the law, and medicine than there are men.

WOMEN ARE IN LOW-PAID AND LOW-STATUS ROLES IN MANY PROFESSIONS

JUDITH BUTLER

1956–

US sociologist and philosopher Judith Butler is one of the world's leading figures in feminism and gender issues. She studied philosophy at Yale University and is currently a professor in Rhetoric and Comparative Literature at the University of California, Berkeley. She is best known for her book *Gender Trouble* (1990), which challenges traditional theories on gender and sexuality. In addition to her academic work, she is also an active campaigner for human rights.

JEWISH HERITAGE

Born in 1956, Butler grew up in a Jewish family in Cleveland, Ohio. According to Butler, she became interested in philosophy at the age of 14 while debating with a rabbi from her local synagogue. Butler's parents were practicing Jews who had lost several family members in the Holocaust. It was her Jewish heritage, she claims, that made her determined to speak out against violence and injustice.

GENDER IDENTITY

In her book *Gender Trouble*, Butler disputes the traditional idea that people are born either as a man or a woman. According to Butler, it is not what people *are*, but what they *do* that determines their gender (she calls this "gender performivity"). In all societies, men and women are expected to behave in either a "masculine" or "feminine" way. After a time, they become so used to repeating these patterns of behavior that their gender seems natural.

> "Masculine and feminine roles are not **biologically** fixed but **socially** constructed."

QUEER THEORY

Butler was influential in developing what came to be known as "Queer Theory," which argues that there is no such thing as "normal" sexuality. She warns against using labels to describe gender and sexuality, arguing that sexual identity can be fluid. As an active campaigner for gay and lesbian human rights, Butler believes that radical action is needed to challenge traditional views on gender issues.

Butler became such a well-known figure in the 1990s that she had her own fanzine called "Judy."

WAR AND THE MEDIA

In her book *Frames of War* (2016), Butler explores how the media portrays the victims of war in a way that distances us from their suffering. She argues that people in Western societies are quick to dismiss victims of war and torture in countries such as Iraq and Syria because their lives and experiences seem so far away. Butler calls for governments and global institutions to ensure that we recognize the suffering of all war victims.

What's my **TRIBE?**

GLOBAL SOCIETY IS A BIG PLACE TO BE AND YOUNG PEOPLE ESPECIALLY CAN FEEL UNSURE OF WHO AND WHERE THEY ARE IN THE WORLD. MANY LIKE THE IDEA OF BEING "DIFFERENT," BUT AT THE SAME TIME LACK CONFIDENCE TO STAND ALONE. BELONGING TO A SMALLER SUBTRIBE PROVIDES AN IDENTITY AND SECURITY.

Every year, fans of comic books, films, and sci fi, often dressed in character, meet at one of the many "Comic-con" events around the world.

We want to belong

Trying to figure out who we are, what we believe in, and how we want the world to see us takes up a lot of emotional energy. One way that people, especially young people, try to deal with all this is to form or join "subcultures." We could perhaps think of these subcultures as small tribes that share a common identity or appearance. Belonging to a subculture provides, at least for a time, answers to the question of who we are. Within such a social group we can find an identity and an enjoyable sense of difference from the norm, not just in terms of the fashions we follow but because of what we believe in and how we interpret and understand the world. Subcultures allow us to associate and socialize with like-minded people who, importantly, understand who we are in a way that the dominant cultures of the world may not.

Goths and geeks

Examples of subcultures can be found everywhere. Some are groups of people who have formed street gangs; many follow a particular style of music such as Punk or Metal. Subcultures like to create "tribal" names for themselves, and sometimes they are given a label by others outside their society.

In the Western world, Goths are a good example of a well-known subculture based around a distinctive type of rock music. Trekkies are a subculture comprising the avid fans of the various Star Trek films and TV series. Attending one of the specialty conventions held around the world is a trekkie's best chance of meeting fellow enthusiasts in the mass, but it takes only a brief conversation for one trekkie to recognize another anywhere. A subculture may also simply mean the supporters of a football

Do you speak Klingon?

You're one of us!

That's my kind of music, too

or baseball team. So each subculture can be radically different from another, but what they all have in common is a desire to stand out in some way from what they see as the mainstream.

Recognizing tribal signs

To identify a subculture, look for the symbols and signs that its members use to communicate their allegiance to a special group. For example, black is a Goth's color of choice for clothes, hair,

> EVERY CULTURE, OR **SUBCULTURE,** IS DEFINED BY A **COMMON SET** OF **VALUES.**
> KENNETH E. BOULDING, BRITISH ECONOMIST

and makeup. Trekkies are fans of "techno-talk" and even learn fictional extraterrestrial languages such as Klingon. But a subculture can be recognizable not just by obscure words or a distinguishing style of dress, but by posture, attitude, and beliefs. A tribal sign could be anything that sends out a message to wider society to say "we are not like you."

GOTHIC GATHERING

Twice a year in Whitby, a clifftop seaside town in the north of England, hundreds of Goths (and thousands of non-Goths) gather for a weekend to celebrate their culture and listen to music. The town's association with Irish author Bram Stoker's classic 1897 gothic horror story *Dracula* provides the attraction. Vampires and the undead are central motifs for the subculture.

From radical to mainstream

Subcultures do not last forever and are absorbed into the mainstream much more quickly than they were in previous decades. What was yesterday's out there and radical is today's sign of conformity. For example, house music that has its subcultural roots in the gay and black communities of Chicago is now a popular dance music for everyone. But however short-lived, subcultures still provide valuable insights into why we are drawn to little tribes and how people create and display a sense of identity.

See also: 14–15, 122–123

Does RACE

One species →
Humans are highly diverse in terms of appearance and lifestyle, but our genes are all more or less the same.

WE BELONG TO A SINGLE SCIENTIFIC CATEGORY...

IN THE 21ST CENTURY, WE MAY WANT TO BELIEVE THAT WE LIVE IN A WORLD WHERE SUPPOSED DIFFERENCES BETWEEN PEOPLE, BASED ON CONSTRUCTED IDEAS OF RACE, HAVE DISAPPEARED. BUT THERE IS EVIDENCE EVERYWHERE—AMONG INDIVIDUALS, IN INSTITUTIONS, AND AT A NATIONAL LEVEL— THAT WE STILL HAVE SOME WAY TO GO.

LAUNDRY IS THE ONLY THING THAT SHOULD BE COLOR SEPARATED.
ANONYMOUS

Focus on ethnicity
In his inaugural speech in 2009, President Obama drew attention to how he was now president in a city where in the past his father had been unable to get work in a restaurant because he was black. Obama was referring to the 1960s, when legally enforceable racial segregation was coming to an end. His presidency was taken to signal the closing of the racial divide in the United States. Events since then have shown that such issues are far from settled. The 2016 US presidential election, the British exit from the European Union (the so-called "Brexit" referendum) in the UK, and the entrance of far-right parties to mainstream politics across Europe, have all highlighted a renewed focus on ethnicity, race, and national identity. So, the answer to "does race matter?" is "yes."

There is more genetic variation within one ethnic group than between different groups.

"Race" does not exist
There is no scientific basis for the term "race." Most humans are genetically very similar and there is so little variation among us that it is not possible to draw neat boundaries around people and label them as a distinct racial group. Race is an example of social construction, where social processes create something that essentially does not exist but takes on real force in people's lives. Sociologists prefer to call these processes "racialization." Historical evidence that race has always been an issue is hard to find.

See also: 50-51, 126-127

matter?

THE HUMAN RACE. ONLY SOCIAL FORCES DIVIDE US.

For example, in ancient Rome there were various leading figures, such as Emperor Septimius Severus (ruled C.E. 193–211), who were black. Little is said of their skin color in accounts written at the time, because the ancient Romans did not think it made any difference. They thought more in terms of judging people as being civilized or a barbarian.

The effects of discrimination

Some sociologists claim that racism is deeply rooted in our society. And, indeed, evidence is found in many spheres of everyday life. People from ethnic minorities are often discriminated against in terms of jobs, housing, and education. Analysis of how racism affects the well-being of minority groups reveals relatively poor health. Where there are lifestyle factors, such as diet, these provide only part of the explanation. Sociologists argue that the chronic stress caused by various forms of racism, including abuse, discrimination, and social stigma, has an even deeper impact on health.

Institutional racism

Institutions such as health care services, police forces, and private companies sometimes treat people differently because of their ethnic origins. This does not mean everyone working for a particular organization is a racist, but that the institution has a culture of negative assumptions about ethnicity. Protest groups formed against institutional racism are part of the 21st-century response to prejudices we have still to consign to the past. Race has not yet ceased to matter.

See also: 91, 102-103 ⊙→

ONLINE ACTIVISTS

The civil rights movement Black Lives Matter was formed in 2013 in response to high-profile police killings of black people in the United States. The group is known globally for its protests against racism. The widely dispersed Black Lives Matter activists are united not under the banner of a single leader but through the far-reaching power of social media platforms such as Facebook and Twitter.

ELIJAH ANDERSON

1943–

US sociologist Elijah Anderson has devoted his career to the issues of race and racism in the inner cities of the United States. Anderson studied sociology at the universities of Indiana and Chicago and is currently a professor at Yale University, where he teaches urban ethnography—the study of city life and culture. Much of his work focuses on the way black people are treated in white middle-class society.

STREET-CORNER LIFE

Anderson was born on a cotton plantation in Mississippi during World War II. After the war, his parents fled the poverty and racism of the South and moved to Chicago. It was here that Anderson first became interested in black street-corner life. He spent three years interviewing local men at a bar on a street corner in Chicago, learning about their community and the way it worked. His research led to his first book, *A Place on the Corner* (1978).

STREET CODES

In his book *Code of the Street* (1999), Anderson claims that many young people dealing with poverty and racism feel a sense of alienation and despair. As a result, they have developed a street "code" that uses violence as a way of gaining respect. Anderson highlights the uneasy relationship between the "street" families who use the code and the "decent" families who work hard and obey the law.

"The **black man** is treated as a dangerous **outsider** until he proves he is worthy of **trust**."

THE GHETTO

In his 2012 article "The Iconic Ghetto," Anderson argues that many racist people in the US regard "the ghetto" (an inner city area where people of a certain race or religion live) as the place where only black people live. They associate the ghetto—and the people who live there—with poverty, drugs, and crime. According to Anderson, many white people believe that black people "belong" in the ghetto, rather than in white middle-class neighborhoods.

THE GHETTO MOMENT

Anderson argues that even though more black people are employed in middle-class professions than ever before, educated and successful black people are still regarded by some as the "exception rather than the rule." He points out that successful black people still experience racist incidents—known as "ghetto moments"—when they are made to feel that they do not belong in white middle-class society.

Anderson experienced his own "ghetto moment" in Cape Cod, when a white man told him to "Go home!"—meaning back to the ghetto.

Who do you **LOVE?**

ALTHOUGH SOCIOLOGY IS THE STUDY OF SOCIETY, IT IS ALSO CONCERNED WITH THE INDIVIDUALS WHO MAKE UP OUR SOCIETY. OUR CHOICE OF PARTNER, FOR EXAMPLE, WHICH MAY SEEM AN ENTIRELY PERSONAL EVENT, IS ACTUALLY INFLUENCED BY THE SOCIETY WE LIVE IN. IF SOCIETY APPROVES OR DISAPPROVES OF OUR CHOICE, IT CAN MAKE US FEEL PART OF SOCIETY OR AN OUTSIDER.

Society and sexuality

It might seem strange to think that society can have an impact on something as intimate and personal as sexuality. Surely feelings of love and desire are natural responses that are triggered when someone feels romantically or sexually attracted to someone else? However, sociologists would say that sexuality, and indeed many other emotional responses and feelings, are strongly influenced by the society in which a person lives.

Society can influence human desire in a number of ways. It can indicate what is an acceptable way to begin dating someone. Do you send them flowers or just press a "like" response on a dating app? Society can also delineate which forms of sexuality are deemed

See also: 50–51, 126–127

❯ A personal choice?
Falling in love seems like the most private thing we can do, but society's approval or disapproval can have an impact even on this part of our lives.

DOES SOCIETY AFFECT WHO WE CHOOSE TO FALL IN LOVE WITH?

See also: 32–33, 39, 143

GAY RIGHTS ARE HUMAN RIGHTS.

HiLLARY CLiNTON, US POLiTiCiAN

acceptable at the current time, such as being straight or gay. It can even shape the expression of emotion and what can and should be said. For example, Valentine's Day, which is celebrated in many countries around the world, brings a social expectation that people will express their love and affection for a partner, or for someone they hope will be their partner, on this day.

> In 2009 Jóhanna Sigurðardóttir became Prime Minister of Iceland, and the world's first openly lesbian leader of a country.

Boxes and labels

Sexuality is not a fixed entity that has always been the same throughout history. In ancient Greece and Rome, for example, people held quite different ideas about sexuality. It was not uncommon for men to have same-sex physical relations with other men. That form of sexual activity was not understood at the time as homosexual.

Indeed, the whole way of thinking that seeks to put people's sexuality into boxes with labels such as straight, gay, or bisexual is something that is very much part of modern life. This idea that everything needs to be put into categories can be traced largely to a historical period known as the Enlightenment, which took place in the 18th century. In his work on human sexuality, French philosopher and sociologist Michel Foucault discovered that the category of "homosexual" only came into being in the 19th century. It was at that time that same-sex attraction began increasingly to be seen as something bad and wrong.

One of the reasons homophobia exists in society is due to what sociologists call "heteronormativity." This is the term for the assumption that heterosexuality is the norm. For example, when someone refers to a partner there is often an assumption is that he or she is of the opposite sex. Heteronormativity is often reinforced by culture and the law. It is worth noting that the right to marry someone of the same sex has only become law in many countries in the early years of this century.

However, perhaps the need to put people in a box is gradually disappearing. Among today's Millennial Generation (born in the 1990s or later) people are increasingly relaxed about their sexuality and sexual identities. That change in attitude among young people does not mean that all societies have become open and accepting of different sexualities. In many parts of the world, people who are attracted to the same sex or are openly gay or lesbian still encounter hostility and discrimination in the form of homophobia.

PROUD TO BE GAY

Gay pride celebrates diversity with parades through cities in many parts of the world. At first, gay pride marches were more political, challenging bigotry and hostility toward gay and lesbian people. The first gay pride took place in June 1970 in Chicago. It marked the anniversary of a riot outside the Stonewall Inn, a gay bar in New York, where patrons fought back against police harassment.

AGE and society

GETTING OLDER IS A FACT OF LIFE. OUR BODIES CHANGE OVER TIME, THE ELASTICITY OF OUR SKIN DECREASES, HAIR THINS AND TURNS GRAY, AND THE TAKEN-FOR-GRANTED ENERGY OF YOUTH REDUCES. ALL HUMANS AGE, BUT WHAT IT IS TO GET OLDER, AND THE EXPERIENCES OF OLDER PEOPLE, DEPEND GREATLY ON THE KIND OF SOCIETY IN WHICH ONE LIVES.

How old is old?

Life expectancy depends on where one is born. In some countries life expectancy is very low because of war, poverty, or the extent of communicable diseases such as HIV/AIDS. In Malawi in Africa, for example, there is an average life expectancy of just under 44 years for both men and women. In Japan, life expectancy is more than 84 years.

The wealth of a country does not mean that its people will live longer. The level of equality, that is the difference between the poorest and the richest people in a society, is important, too. So, in Norway, which has a very equal society, the life expectancy is nearly 82 years; while in the US, which has a fairly unequal society, it is nearer to 79 years.

In some countries the population is aging, so the experience of older people is of increasing importance. In Britain the over 65s outnumber those under 16, and in Japan there has been a surge in the elderly population.

How old age is seen

The way different societies view old age also varies. The visible signs of aging— the gray hair and lines on the skin—have been interpreted in different ways by societies at different times. For example, it was socially desirable to appear more mature in Victorian England (1837–1901) and young men would try to make themselves look older by growing beards as soon as they could. In present-day North America and Europe, where youth is highly valued, a wide range of technologies exist, including painful medical procedures, that can help people maintain a youthful appearance by hiding the natural signs of aging. Singaporean sociologist Angelique Chan notes that in Malay cultures where religious wisdom is prized, older people enjoy a reasonable social status. However, in countries like China that prize people who are earning money, being older is not so valued.

A golden time?

British sociologist Paul Higgs has been interested in studying what it is to be older in wealthy countries across Western

OLDER RUNNERS

French sociologist Emmanuelle Tulle's research on older competitive runners challenged stereotypes about older people. In her work with runners in their 40s, 50s, and 60s, she found that they had developed an urge to run over many years. Despite being older, their motivation was not to prevent illness, neither did they want to be seen as heroes of old age; they just wanted to run without being dismissed as foolish.

According to the United Nations, by 2050 the global population of people over 60 will be 2.1 billion.

See also: 39

Europe and North America. His research has taken him away from stereotypical views that old age should be seen as a low point in people's lives. He sees older age as being a "golden time" for many older people alive today—a time when they can enjoy pursuing the activities, goals, and dreams they did not have the time to realize when they were younger.

However, it may be different for today's young people. The generation that Higgs refers to grew up in a time of economic and social stability. British journalists Ed Howker and Shiv Malik in their book *Jilted Generation* (2013) and US sociologist Jennifer Silva in her book *Coming Up Short: Working-Class Adulthood in an Age of Uncertainty* (2013) have argued that today's young people lack the same job security and finances to buy a home that were available for previous generations. They might be the first generation whose standard of living will be lower than that of their parents. When they get older their lives could be marked by inequality and poverty.

So society's view of what it is to be old is evolving and depends on economic as well as cultural factors.

OLDER AGE CAN BE A TIME OF GREATER FREEDOM

New things
Getting older can be a time to explore new pastimes and pursue dreams that were put on hold during busier times.

PERHAPS MY BEST YEARS ARE GONE... BUT I WOULDN'T WANT THEM BACK. NOT WITH THE FIRE IN ME NOW.

SAMUEL BECKETT, IRISH PLAYWRIGHT

What does **FAMILY** mean?

THE FAMILY IS OFTEN SEEN AS THE BUILDING BLOCK OF SOCIETY. A CHILD'S EXPERIENCE OF FAMILY, WHETHER GOOD OR BAD, SHAPES HIS OR HER WHOLE LIFE. THE FAMILY SHOULD BE A STABLE PLACE FOR CHILDREN TO LEARN THE BEHAVIOR AND VALUES OF SOCIETY. HOWEVER, THE IMAGE OF THE FAMILY IS EVOLVING, AND THESE DAYS FAMILIES COME IN MANY DIFFERENT FORMS.

See also: 28–29

Family values

The family is regarded as being at the heart of society. It is seen as a safe and secure place where children are brought up. As such, the family acts as an important agent of socialization, the process by which the norms (what is regarded as the acceptable way to behave) and values of a society are passed from one generation to another.

However, the family can also have a negative side. Sometimes, it can be a place of abuse and violence, and an area where partners exert control over one another, or their children. Given the importance and complexity of the family, sociologists have long been interested in trying to both understand what the family is and examine how the family has changed over time.

In 2015, there were 2.2 million marriages in the US and 800,000 divorces.

A perfect family

US sociologist Talcott Parsons carried out one of the most influential sociological studies of the family unit in the 1950s. He was interested in the role that the family played in making society work smoothly. For him, the family was a place where children learned the values of their society and where the emotional needs of the adult were taken care of. He also thought that it was best that the husband took on the role of earning the money for the family, while the wife stayed at home and looked after the emotional needs of the family. In many ways Talcott's work reflects the time in which he was writing. The American family of the 1950s had an idealized "apple pie" image of family life (the stereotypical happy mom and dad with two perfect children). In fact, this image of a "traditional" family has not always existed.

NO ONE TO BLAME

Most divorces these days are "no fault" divorces, meaning that neither partner is blamed for the breakdown of the marriage, a situation that is better for both parties and any children involved. At certain times in history, divorces were only granted when one partner had committed adultery, been violent, or was mentally ill.

In industrial societies of the 19th century, poorer people, including children, worked long hours, which meant that they hardly saw each other, and it was feared that the working-class family might disappear.

Different forms of family

Changes in family life make it hard to talk of "the family" as a fixed thing. Perhaps it is better to use the term "families" to allow for the idea that there are many different forms of family these days. "Blended" or "reconstituted" families where children live with a stepparent and stepsiblings are increasingly common. This kind of family forms when adults make a new relationship after the ending of a previous one, often following a divorce.

Other family forms include same-sex relationships, which can include children. The slow, but steady trend in accepting gay and lesbian families as part of mainstream society has followed the legalizing of same-sex marriage and civil partnerships in many European countries and some states in the US. While there are many different ways that people form intimate relationships, what is striking is that most people still opt for some kind of long-term relationship with a partner, and frequently with children. These may not last "till death us do part," as in previous times, but families seem likely to endure as social forms.

Family forms ➜
Relationships change so that children may grow up with a stepparent or single parent or with parents in a same-sex partnership.

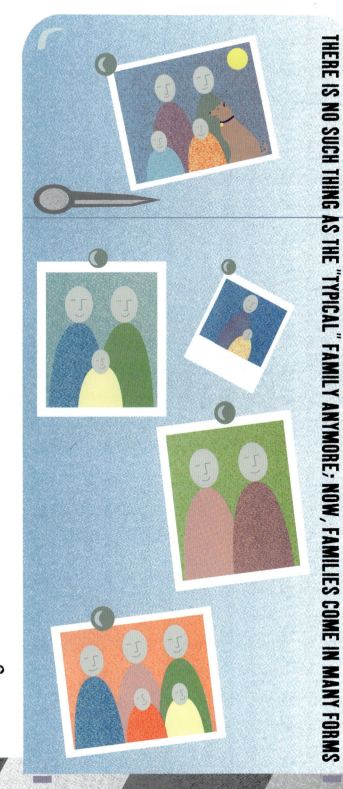

THERE IS NO SUCH THING AS THE "TYPICAL" FAMILY ANYMORE; NOW, FAMILIES COME IN MANY FORMS

WHEN THE DISCIPLINE OF SOCIOLOGY WAS FORMING IN THE EARLY 19TH CENTURY, CLASS WAS ONE OF THE MOST FREQUENTLY DISCUSSED TOPICS. WHAT IS MEANT BY CLASS, HOW DIFFERENT CLASSES ARE DEFINED, AND WHETHER CLASS STILL EXISTS ARE SUBJECTS THAT ARE STILL HOTLY DEBATED BY MANY SOCIOLOGISTS TODAY.

THE HISTORY OF ALL HITHERTO EXISTING SOCIETY IS THE HISTORY OF CLASS STRUGGLE.
KARL MARX

⚙ Acting middle class
Although class distinctions may be less clear-cut these days, the class system itself has not disappeared. Having money, knowing the right people, and having middle-class manners can bring many benefits.

DO WE ALL DREAM OF A MIDDLE-CLASS LIFE?

Are we all MIDDLE

Different views of class
Early sociological thinkers Max Weber, Karl Marx, and Émile Durkheim all wrote about class. Marx is well-known for his writings on the subject, which describe a divide in society between the ruling class, the profit-seeking owners of businesses, and the people they exploited, the working class, who were employed in the factories. Weber agreed with Marx that class existed but also noted that the differences were not only economic. Some jobs, such as being a minister or priest, were poorly paid but carried a

high social status. Other jobs offered little wealth but, because they made someone an elected state official, they brought considerable power. For Durkheim, however, the allocation of people to different classes, based on their abilities, was essential to the smooth running of society.

48% of people in the US define themselves as working class.

Does class still exist?
All three were writing about society in the mid-19th to early 20th centuries. It was easier then to identify class differences. There were sharp divisions between working-class manual laborers who worked amid the grime of the

factory floor and middle-class, non-manual workers, who worked in clean offices. But is it easy to define the classes today? In 1996, Australian Jan Pakulski and Briton Malcolm Waters claimed in their work *The Death of Class* that class has disappeared in modern society. They argued that globalization, a reduction in the concentration of wealth, and the decline of traditional industries has made the concept of class irrelevant. They claimed that today, differences between social classes are based on status, and this is indicated by the ownership of consumer goods: the clothes you wear, the phone you have, and so on.

Class is not just about money

However, class appears to be more resilient than Pakulski and Waters thought. Looking at events since the mid-1990s, society has actually become more unequal (see pp114–115) and two major events in 2016, the EU referendum ("Brexit") in the UK and the US presidential election, appeared to show that class identity and class issues are very much alive. Both results revealed a working class that did not feel represented by a political elite and voted to change it.

See also: 44–45,100–101

CLASS now?

BLUE OR WHITE?

The terms "blue-collar," meaning someone who is working class, and "white-collar," meaning a middle-class office worker, come from the clothing traditionally worn in the workplace. The blue coveralls that manual workers wore tended not to show dirt or grease, while office workers favored white shirts and blouses. Today these terms act as a useful shorthand.

French sociologist Pierre Bourdieu (1930–2002) argued that class was still important. He offered a more nuanced understanding of how differences between social classes remain. Class distinctions, for Bourdieu, are composed of the combination of three different forms of capital. The first is economic capital, or how much money someone has. The second is social capital, meaning the connections people have to resources such as money and jobs. The third is cultural capital, which refers to knowing how to behave (such as how to speak, what clothes to wear) in certain situations. The debate will continue, but it seems that class identities have not disappeared.

KARL MARX

1818–1883

Karl Marx was born in Trier, Germany, the son of a successful lawyer. He studied law at the University of Berlin, although he was more interested in history and philosophy. In 1843, he moved to Paris, where he met several leading socialists, including Friedrich Engels, with whom he wrote *The Communist Manifesto*. Regarded as one of the founding fathers of sociology, Marx was also an influential economist, philosopher, and historian, whose writings have inspired political movements around the world.

THE PURSUIT OF PROFIT

Marx's most famous work, *Das Kapital*, examines the nature and development of capitalist societies. The first volume was published in 1857; two more volumes appeared after his death. In *Das Kapital*, Marx argues that working people are exploited in a capitalist society and that human labor has become a "commodity." According to Marx, it is the relentless pursuit of profit and wealth that defines capitalism as a social system.

CLASS CONFLICT

Marx stated that a capitalist society could be divided into two distinct classes: the working class (proletariat) and the ruling class (bourgeoisie). He argued that the ruling classes, who owned the businesses and gained the profits, exploited the working classes, who were forced to sell their skills and labor in order to survive. Marx believed that conflict between the two classes was inevitable and that the working class would eventually overthrow the capitalist system and ultimately establish communism.

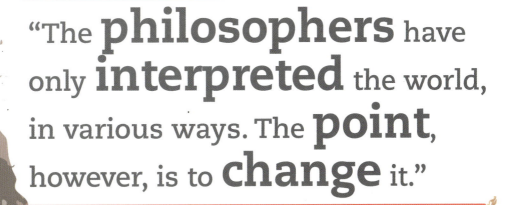

"The **philosophers** have only **interpreted** the world, in various ways. The **point**, however, is to **change** it."

Marx spent most of his life in poverty, relying on support from Friedrich Engels, whose family had made their fortune in the textile industry.

A LIFE IN EXILE

Having been forced to leave Germany in 1843 because of his radical views, Marx spent the rest of his life in exile, first moving to Paris and then to Brussels. He was expelled from Belgium shortly after the publication of *The Communist Manifesto* in 1848. In 1849, he and his family moved to London where he wrote *Das Kapital*. After the death of his wife in 1881, his health deteriorated. Marx died in 1883, and is buried in Highgate Cemetery in London.

A SENSE OF ALIENATION

Throughout his work, Marx was concerned with the emotional and physical costs of living in a capitalist society. He believed that many people experience a feeling of "alienation"—a sense of being unfulfilled in life and disconnected from other people. Marx believed that this feeling of alienation was especially common in the workplace, where people felt they had no control over their working conditions or the goods they produced.

GENDER IDENTITY

Some of the first feminist writing was by British academic Mary Wollstonecraft in 1792. In her book, *A Vindication of the Rights of Women*, she argues that women should be educated. Over time, feminist writers challenged other social conventions. French philosopher Simone de Beauvoir's key feminist text, *The Second Sex* (1949), questions the notion of natural gender difference.

In 1867, Karl Marx publishes the first volume of his best-known work, *Das Kapital*. In it, he outlines how the system of capitalism creates different social classes in society. The owners of factories were known as the bourgeoisie, and those who worked in them, the proletariat. There have been many other studies of class since then.

AN ANALYSIS OF CLASS

Identity
IN CONTEXT

BLACK IDENTITY

W. E .B. Du Bois published *The Souls of Black Folk* in 1904. In it, he is strongly critical of the marginalization (pushing to the side) and undermining of African-American culture and identity. His work is one of a sequence of events in the US that lead to greater equality for African Americans.

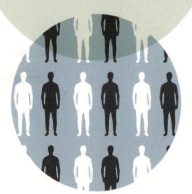

The notion of childhood as a special and innocent time of life is a recent social construction. French historian Phillipe Ariès' book, *Centuries of Childhood*, was published in English in 1962 and explained how childhood as we know it did not exist until the 19th century. Before this, people were either infants or adults.

CHILDHOOD

In 2015, the United Nations noted that the number of older people is steadily rising. By 2050, it is estimated that there will be 2.1 billion older people—60 years or over—up from 901 million in 2015. What it means to be older is changing. From being a marginalized group in society, older people are increasingly becoming more central.

LIVING LONGER

Identity is not made up of just one factor, such as class or gender. Who we are emerges from the combination of several aspects. In the 1980s, US sociologist bell hooks wrote about what she called "intersectionality" which was based on her experiences as an African-American woman.

INTERSECTIONALITY

Sociology can tell us a lot about how people's identities are formed. There are aspects of our identity we can choose, and others on which the society in which we live exerts a great deal of influence. Key issues include social class, gender, sexuality, and race and, as we live even longer, age.

SUBCULTURES

In *Resistance Through Rituals* (1975), edited by Stuart Hall and Tony Jefferson, the authors look at what young people are trying to communicate through music-based subcultures. The book deals with subcultures of the time such as Mods, Skinheads, and Rude Boys. Research since then has explored other youth subcultures.

RISE OF GAY RIGHTS

The Gay Rights movement can be traced back to events in Greenwich Village, New York, in 1969. The Stonewall Inn was a popular venue for gay and lesbian people at a time when being gay and lesbian was illegal and culturally unacceptable. One night, when faced with a police raid, people fought back. This was the starting point for gay liberation.

Does society EXIST?

What do schools TEACH?

Are INSTITUTIONS a good thing?

Who holds the POWER?

What role does RELIGION play in society?

Does RELIGION still MATTER?

RURAL life versus URBAN life

A sense of COMMUNITY

WHY do we WORK?

HOW is work CHANGING?

WATCHING the workers

All societies need institutions, such as the law, communities, business, and religion to help them run more smoothly. These are the foundations upon which our society is built. Other institutions such as the family and education help to prepare people to be part of society. How these social structures affect us and how they are changing are of great interest to sociologists.

What do schools TEACH?

DO STUDENTS LEARN ONLY WHAT IS ON THE SCHOOL CURRICULUM? SOCIOLOGISTS HAVE VARIED IDEAS ABOUT WHAT YOUNG PEOPLE REALLY EXPERIENCE IN THE CLASSROOM. IS EDUCATION MEANT TO FILL US WITH USEFUL INFORMATION, PROVIDE SOCIAL CONTACTS— OR JUST PREPARE US FOR THE WORKPLACE?

In 2015, researchers at the University of Oxford, UK, recommended a 10am start for the school day, to allow young people more sleep.

Understanding education

In many countries, young people are in full-time education between the ages of five and 18, or longer if they go on to college. Both students and their parents usually see education as a phase in life when young people acquire knowledge and skills that enable them to discover what interests them and to find jobs. But sociologists have more complicated views on education.

The hidden curriculum

In a classic work on education, *Schooling in Capitalist America*, published in 1976, US sociologists Samuel Bowles and Herbert Gintis suggest that while education does provide knowledge and skills, it also has a role in maintaining the existing social order. Education accustoms young people to accepting certain behaviors and restrictions; in other words, it makes them do what they are told.

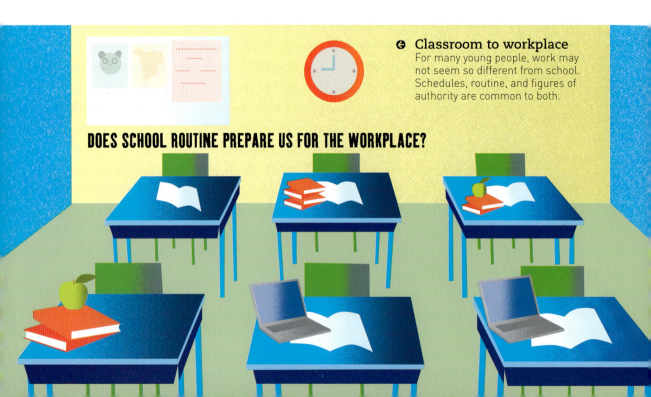

⊖ Classroom to workplace
For many young people, work may not seem so different from school. Schedules, routine, and figures of authority are common to both.

DOES SCHOOL ROUTINE PREPARE US FOR THE WORKPLACE?

In their book, Bowles and Gintis explained what they called the "hidden curriculum." This has nothing to do with the formal curriculum of studies that every student learns, with subjects such as mathematics, science, and languages. The hidden curriculum uses rules, punishments, and rewards to teach students to conform to such norms (social expectations) as punctuality, dress codes, and obedience to instructions from those in authority.

Bowles and Gintis claimed that there is a parallel between the way school is organized and the way work is organized. In what they called a "correspondence theory," they saw the power of teachers as similar to that of a manager at work, and the routine of school corresponding with the nine-to-five routine of the workplace. Neither students nor workers have much control over what they do.

Gaining and losing

French sociologist Pierre Bourdieu, in his analysis of education in the 1980s and 1990s, thought schools were important as places where people acquire useful contacts and join social networks: gaining what he called "social capital." He claimed that students also acquired "cultural capital," by which he meant they learned how to behave in society. However, social and cultural capital vary by social class and act as a means of maintaining class distinctions. Bourdieu noted that the social and cultural capital provided by expensive private schools helped the rich to stay rich but excluded children from more ordinary backgrounds.

Following on from Bourdieu, US social scientist Garth Stahl looked at the education of white working-class boys in England. His research, published in 2015, found that the modern schools in his study concentrated on individual ambition and competitiveness. Many working-class boys were uncomfortable with such ideals, rather identifying themselves as a group where equality and sticking together mattered more than standing out. As a result, the boys felt devalued and on the margins of school culture. Stahl believes this is why working-class boys often do not do well at school.

There are many ways in which education is a preparation for adult society and the world of work. It appears that much of what we learn is not part of a formal classroom schedule.

See also: 100–101

EDUCATION MUST NOT SIMPLY TEACH **WORK**—IT MUST TEACH **LIFE.**
W. E .B. DU BOIS, US SOCIOLOGIST

Are **INSTITUTIONS** a good thing?

SOCIETY IS MADE UP OF MORE THAN THE RANDOM ACTIONS OF INDIVIDUALS MAKING THEIR WAY THROUGH LIFE IN DIFFERENT WAYS. INSTEAD, OUR LIVES HAVE A STRUCTURE AND THE SOCIETY WE LIVE IN HAS ORDER. THIS IS DUE TO THE INSTITUTIONS, OR BUILDING BLOCKS OF SOCIETY, THINGS SUCH AS EDUCATION, RELIGION, THE FAMILY, AND THE LAW.

See also: 32–33

We need structure

Sociologists have observed that society has a range of structures or "institutions" that give pattern and form to people's lives. In sociology an institution does not necessarily refer to a building but rather to the ways of doing things that are governed by sets of rules (or "norms" and "values" in sociological language). These rules may be official rules that are laid down by an organization (the Church, a workplace, or the government, for example) or they may be informal rules that individuals have come up with. It does not really matter if they are official or unofficial as long as people agree to them and stick to them. By doing so, people's lives are given some form of shape and meaningful order. Without them, things would fall apart and people would struggle to know what to do or how to behave.

Foundations of society

Social institutions provide the necessary stability and structure to make society possible. They are both the foundation and the building blocks of society. In a book called *The Social Construction of Reality* published in 1966, Austrian sociologists Peter Berger and Thomas Luckmann noted that institutions played a key role in maintaining society. They argue that we often take institutions for granted and do not really notice them, but they play a vital role in giving shape to the society in

PART OF THE INSTITUTION

In his book *Asylums* (1961), US sociologist Erving Goffman investigated the issue of "institutionalization." This applied to people in prisons, long-term hospitals, or mental health facilities, where the institution became so dominant in their lives that they could not eat, sleep, dress, or play without the routine laid down by the institution.

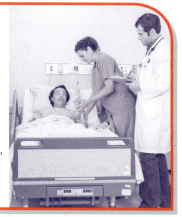

EDUCATION

GOVERNMENT

RELIGION

BUSINESS

FAMILY

LAW

MEDIA

CULTURE

which we live. Institutions also affect people's identities, shaping in various ways how they think and act toward others.

In the US only 4.4% of the top 500 companies have women CEOs. In the UK there are 7 women CEOs in the top 100 companies.

Structures of inequality?

The most common types of institutions across all societies are education, religion, the family, marriage, government, culture, and business. Even though sociologists agree that institutions play an essential part in maintaining social order, they understand that institutions affect different groups in different ways. Some sociologists who come from a Marxist, feminist, or anti-racist background see institutions as ways of maintaining exploitation and oppression. For example, a feminist might see business institutions as supporting men's privileged position—indicated by the low number of women in top management and by the fact that women have lower-paid jobs.

> **NO MAN EVER LOOKS AT THE WORLD WITH PRISTINE EYES. HE SEES IT EDITED BY A DEFINITE SET OF CUSTOMS AND INSTITUTIONS...**
>
> **RUTH BENEDICT, US ANTHROPOLOGIST**

Others would see institutions as essential devices holding our society together and giving us rules to live by. Without them, they argue, there would be chaos and confusion.

During the 2016 US presidential election, Republican Donald Trump and Democrat Bernie Sanders both claimed that US political and economic institutions were not working. Coming from very different political positions and offering different solutions, they each stated that the institutions were biased to maintain the wealth of an elite and were letting down the majority of ordinary people.

See also: 50–51, 76–77

CHARLES WRIGHT MILLS

1916–1962

Born in Texas, Charles Wright Mills was a hugely influential social thinker. He studied sociology at the University of Texas and was a professor of sociology at Columbia University until his death from a heart attack at the age of 45. Influenced by the ideas of Max Weber, he believed that sociology should be used to bring about social change. He is best known for his work on social inequality, class structure, and the nature of power.

THE NEW MIDDLE CLASS

Wright Mills was particularly interested in the changing nature of the middle classes in the United States. In his book *White Collar*, published in 1951, he claimed that "white-collar" workers, who are workers employed in offices, had lost touch with traditional values, such as pride in craftsmanship. While enjoying the benefits provided by white-collar jobs, the middle classes had little control over their lives and had become uninterested in political and social affairs.

THE POWERFUL FEW

In his book *The Power Elite*, published in 1956, Wright Mills analyzed the way a small minority of political, business, and military leaders—the power elite—were able to dominate US society. He pointed out that ordinary people in "mass society" are unaware that only a small number of individuals are responsible for the decisions that affect their everyday lives.

In 1960, Wright Mills went to Cuba to find out about the Cuban revolution. He interviewed revolutionary leader Fidel Castro.

SOCIOLOGICAL IMAGINATION

In *The Sociological Imagination*, published 1959, Wright Mills explored how the private problems of an individual are linked to wider social issues. When a worker is laid off, the problem is a private one—it affects the individual who is now unemployed. However, a firm's decision to cut staff is usually based on wider social and economic developments, such as increased taxes or the cost of raw materials.

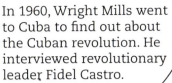

"Neither the **life** of an individual nor the **history** of a society can be **understood** without understanding **both**."

A LETTER OF HOPE

Wright Mills believed that sociologists should use their knowledge to change and improve society. His ideas influenced several social movements in the United States during the 1960s. In 1960, he wrote an open letter to the political movement known as the "New Left" that paved the way for wider changes in the law on issues such as gay rights, abortion, and gender equality.

See also: 18–19, 36–37

Who holds the POWER?

POWER IS THE ABILITY TO INFLUENCE, CONTROL, OR MANIPULATE OTHER PEOPLE. SOCIOLOGISTS ARE INTERESTED IN WHO HAS POWER, WHY THEY HAVE IT, AND HOW THEY USE IT. POWER CAN BE EXERCISED IN THE WORKPLACE OR THE HOME, AS WELL AS IN MANY OTHER SUBTLE WAYS THROUGHOUT SOCIETY.

The power of employment

One of the founders of social science, Karl Marx, saw that power was held by a small, unelected elite in society. They held that power because they owned, in his words, the "means of production," and by this he meant that they owned businesses. Today, this elite are the owners of big businesses and the chief executive officers (CEOs) who run companies. This business class is an influential force in society because it has the power to give people jobs or take them away, and without a job it is difficult to survive financially and socially. People find it hard to pay their rent or mortgage, socialize with friends and family, and they may feel very unhappy.

Marx noted that ordinary people, the workers, also possess a great deal of power, only they do not realize they have it. He argued that if working people joined together they could resist the power of the capitalists. This is how trade unions work. By joining forces and having the option to go on strike, if necessary, workers can challenge the power of employers to set low wages and offer unsatisfactory working conditions.

Men's power over women

In a different sphere of society, British feminist Sylvia Walby, in her influential book *Theorizing Patriarchy* (1990), marked out six ways that men had power over women. First, in the home, with women doing most of the mundane household chores. Second, in the workplace, where women tend to do the majority of low-status and low-paid jobs. Third, by the state, who make laws and policies that benefit men over women. Fourth, by male violence, when men use their power to physically and mentally intimidate women. Fifth, by control over sexuality, with the needs of heterosexual males given priority over other sexual preferences. Finally, sixth, in most areas of culture, male interests take preference over women's. An example is in athletics, where sports played by men dominate the media.

Arrangements of power

French sociologist and philosopher, Michel Foucault, was interested in how power is used, particularly on a day-to-day basis in people's lives. Foucault claims that power is not exercised by a strong figure using physical force as it would have been in the Middle Ages. In modern society power takes on a more subtle form. People are controlled by the way that space and time are organized in society, which makes people's bodies and minds comply with dominant ideas. Think of how

There are only two women in the list of the top ten most powerful people in the world.

WHERE THERE IS POWER THERE IS RESISTANCE.

MICHEL FOUCAULT, FRENCH PHILOSOPHER AND SOCIOLOGIST

HOW MUCH CONTROL DO YOU REALLY HAVE OVER YOUR LIFE ?

Who's in charge? ➲
Even in our own homes we cannot do just what we want. We must abide by the laws of our country and by the rules of our society, such as not leaving children unattended.

See also: 100–101 ➡

a school classroom is arranged: the way chairs and tables are set out creates a power relationship where the teacher can oversee what the students are doing and regulate who does what and when. There is also a strict timetable dictating when and where students have to be.

However, Foucault also famously notes that where there is power there is also resistance. What he means is that people will not always go along with what they are told to do or how they are told to behave, and they may take to the streets to protest or even to riot.

WORLD'S MOST POWERFUL
Russian president Vladimir Putin has topped the *Forbes* Power List for three years as the most powerful person in the world. His actions have an impact on people not just in Russia but around the world. Putin's career began in 1975 when he joined the KGB (the old Soviet security service) and he became president in 2000. He presents a tough, physically strong, rather stereotypical, male image.

What role does RELIGION play in society?

SOCIOLOGISTS ARE NOT NECESSARILY INTERESTED IN WHETHER A GOD OR DIVINE BEING ACTUALLY EXISTS. INSTEAD, THE EMPHASIS IN SOCIOLOGY IS ON HOW RELIGIONS RELATE TO WIDER SOCIETY, HOW THEY SHAPE SOCIETY, AND ARE, IN TURN, SHAPED BY IT.

Religion is a social glue

Two of the founding figures in sociology, Durkheim (see pp 74–75) and Marx (see pp 36–37), offer two quite different interpretations of the place of religion in society. Both were writing at times of great social upheaval in the 19th and early 20th centuries and pondered what religion is for and why it maintained a presence amid all the change. In his extensive study of religions, Émile Durkheim always maintained that there are plenty of world religions, such as Buddhism and Jainism, that are not centered on a divine being or beings, but rather emphasize certain preferred behaviors. For Durkheim, religion acts as a form of social glue, maintaining social cohesion and binding people together, by sharing and affirming the beliefs, values, and norms of a society.

Hartford Institute for Religion Research found that more than 40% of Americans say they go to church, but less than 20% actually do.

See also: 44–45

> # FULFILMENT OF WORLDLY DUTIES IS...THE ONLY WAY TO LIVE ACCEPTABLY TO GOD.
>
> **MAX WEBER, GERMAN SOCIOLOGIST**

A part of something bigger

Durkheim explained that sacred objects and sacred rituals associated with religions kept their special qualities because they were imbued with significance by society. They contained no built-in powers or link to a divine being in themselves. So, when people are engaged in acts of religious worship they are not actually looking up to a divine being, a god, but rather worshiping the values of their own society. The act of worship is important as it provides what Durkheim refers to as "emotional effervescence" or an upswelling of feelings that helps people to commit to their society and feel they are part of something bigger than

SHARING A FAITH WITH OTHERS BINDS A COMMUNITY TOGETHER. THE RITUALS MAY SERVE ONLY TO STRENGTHEN THE LINKS WITH OTHERS IN THE COMMUNITY, RATHER THAN HAVING ANY SPECIAL POWERS OF THEIR OWN.

See also: 52–53, 75

RELIGION OFFERS COMFORT IN AN UNCERTAIN WORLD

themselves. He recognized that people are not just rational machines, but instead require activities and moments in their lives when they need to connect emotionally with others around them.

Religion is a painkiller

Karl Marx offered a different perspective. For him religion provides a means of dealing with the pain and suffering created by living in an alienating and exploitative capitalist society. Christianity's promise of a better life to come provides comfort. The idea is that the problems one is facing now will be made better at some future point. That notion of comfort informs Marx's widely known but misunderstood observation that "...religion is the opium of the people." What he did not mean was that people were addicted to religion. In his day, the mid-1800s, opium was used as painkiller and a drug that helped people deal with the sufferings of life. If he was writing today Marx might have said that "religion is the Prozac of

the masses," Prozac being a form of medication that helps with depression. For Marx, religion is ultimately an illusory solution to humanity's issues. Real change lies in radically transforming the present world as opposed to waiting for salvation in an afterlife that does not exist.

Although Durkheim and Marx were writing a long time ago, their ideas are still relevant. Religion and ritual provide some form of structure in many people's lives and give them the opportunity to feel part of something. Religion can also offer a sense of security and hope for the future in a difficult and uncertain world.

PROTESTANT WORK ETHIC
German theologian Martin Luther suggested that working hard and earning a living was a way to fulfill one's duties to God. This idea became part of the belief system of Protestants, and is described by Max Weber in his book *The Protestant Work Ethic and the Spirit of Capitalism* in 1905. Weber saw this spiritual "work ethic" as the drive to build wealth behind modern capitalist economies.

Does RELIGION

There are about 488 million followers of Buddhism worldwide. It is sometimes called a philosophy rather than a religion.

A BIG QUESTION FACING SOCIOLOGISTS TODAY IS WHETHER OR NOT RELIGION IS IN DECLINE. ARE WE BECOMING A SECULAR SOCIETY, ONE THAT IS NONRELIGIOUS? IF WE ARE, IT COULD MARK A MAJOR CHANGE IN HOW PEOPLE VIEW SOCIETY AND THEIR PLACE IN IT, AS WELL AS HOW THEY ADDRESS THE DEEPER QUESTIONS ABOUT THE MEANING OF LIFE.

Science replaces religion

Sociologists are interested in any changes in society, and this includes looking at secularization, which is the process by which a society becomes less religious and people start to be less attached to religious ideas. The beginning of the decline of religion in Europe can be attributed to a time in history called the Enlightenment. During this period of the 17th and 18th centuries, great intellectual and scientific innovations took place in Europe. The Enlightenment challenged the religious beliefs that had been the dominant way of understanding the world. Instead of referring to the Bible as a way to explain all aspects of life, now explanations came from the study of science. This undermined the authority of the Church and began the process of questioning the existence of God.

Do you go to church?

Many of the early sociologists—Max Weber, Karl Marx, and Émile Durkheim—thought that we were moving toward a secular society. This idea seems to be supported by current statistics measuring church attendance. For example, the Church of England published statistics in 2016 showing that church attendance is half of what it was in the 1960s, and attendances at Sunday services are now below one million people—less than 2% of

MANY STILL HAVE RELIGIOUS FEELINGS...

ALTHOUGH FEWER PEOPLE GO TO CHURCH

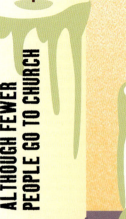

still MATTER?

the population. In the US, according to the Hartford Institute of Religion Research, more than 40 percent of Americans "say" they go to church weekly, In reality, however, less than 20 percent actually do. Throughout Western Europe and North America, the trend toward a more secular society and a decline in church attendance appears to be fairly conclusive.

However, a decline in attendance does not necessarily mean that religion is withering away. While some people may declare themselves atheists (people who do not believe in God), others say they are agnostic, meaning that they are not so sure. Many people express a sense of spirituality, such as a belief that there is some power greater than themselves. This feeling may not be focused on God, as it is in Christianity, Islam, or Judaism, but could be expressed in terms of alternative beliefs. So, people may turn away from mainstream religion, but that does not mean that they do not retain religious feelings.

Also, other religions around the world are prospering. Islam is the second largest religion in the world and gaining adherents in many different countries.

⚘ The flame still burns
Although fewer people attend worship services than in the past, Christianity and other faiths have endured. There are also people who prefer not to belong to any particular faith but still believe in a power greater than themselves.

SECULAR "CHURCH"
The Sunday Assembly meets regularly in cities around the world. It may look like a conventional church assembly—someone stands at the front and leads the meeting, people stand and sing songs—but there are crucial differences. It is a secular congregation, the songs are pop songs, the sermons are talks about social issues, and most significantly, it is nonreligious.

A "low-level" belief
Australian sociologist Bryan Turner shifted the emphasis away from the question of whether religion is disappearing from society, to look at how religion is experienced by people today. In this book, *Religion and Modern Society* (2011), he refers to a "low-level religion," which recognizes that religion still informs people's lives, but not in the way it once did, when it was a dominant "high-level" presence in people's lives involving regular church attendance, social events, and guidance from religious leaders. Religion remains a significant part of life for some, but for many, it exists as a more informal, private experience.

See also: 59, 68

> **RELIGION IS THE SIGH OF THE OPPRESSED CREATURE. THE HEART OF A HEARTLESS WORLD... THE OPIUM OF THE PEOPLE.**
>
> **KARL MARX**

RURAL life versus

THE WORLD REACHED AN HISTORIC MILESTONE IN 2009. FOR THE FIRST TIME EVER MORE PEOPLE ARE LIVING IN URBAN AREAS THAN IN RURAL LOCATIONS. REACHING THIS POINT HAS BEEN THE RESULT OF VARIOUS CHANGES TAKING PLACE, AT DIFFERENT RATES, IN DIFFERENT PARTS OF THE WORLD.

THE CITY IS A STATE OF MIND...
ROBERT E. PARK, US SOCIOLOGIST

Move to the cities

In Europe, the Industrial Revolution of the 19th century caused massive changes to society as the new factories producing textiles encouraged people to move to the cities from the countryside to find work. Cities such as Manchester, England, one of the main centers of the Industrial Revolution, saw the population triple between 1811 and 1851 from just over 100,000 to 300,000. In other parts of the world, the process of urbanization has happened more recently, but much more rapidly. The population of Lagos, Nigeria, for example, increased from 1.4 million in 1971 to somewhere near 21 million by 2016.

The population shift during the Industrial Revolution attracted the attention of German sociologist Ferdinand Tönnies. Writing in the late

> Tokyo, Japan is ranked the largest city in the world by land area, population, and density.

19th century, he speculated that the fabric of society would change considerably, if not fall apart altogether, with this move to urban living.

Gemeinschaft and Gesellschaft

Tönnies put forward two concepts that can be used to explain the differences between rural and urban living. The first is *Gemeinschaft*, usually translated into English as "community," but in the original German it carries connotations of deep human bonds, empathy, and shared values. This contrasts with *Gesellschaft*. Again, the English translation of "association" does not quite capture the original meaning of a more rational, functional, and anonymous way of interacting with people. However, if you think of how people shy away from contact behind books, newspapers, or cell phones on the subway in New York or the U-Bahn in Berlin, that should give you an idea of what the concept means.

In the past, it was often assumed that one could only find communities, or *Gemeinschaft*, in rural locations where people lived in small villages, not in large-scale, impersonal cities. However, research has proved that to be incorrect. Park and Wirth (commonly known as The Chicago School), who conducted research between 1920 to 1940 in the US city of Chicago, found that "urban villages" existed. These were small communities living in big cities that featured strong bonds between people that had traditionally been associated with

A RIGHT TO THE CITY

In the 1960s, French sociologist Henri Lefebvre was concerned that the modern urban environment excluded certain groups—who were users of the city—in favor of those who owned property or were influential in other ways. He wanted everyone to have a "right to the city," meaning a say in how it was run and access to its resources.

URBAN life

rural village life. In England, Willmott and Young's 1950s research in Bethnal Green, London, also found a thriving working-class community in an inner-city location. Built around strong women, residents enjoyed a sense of neighborliness and would frequently step in to help each other out.

Poverty and innovation

One current area of interest for sociologists is the growth of informal settlements, or slums, in countries such as India, Brazil, and Nigeria. People seeking to escape poverty in rural areas move to the city in the hope of finding security and employment in emerging megacites such as Mumbai, Rio de Janeiro, or Lagos. These informal settlements can be contradictory places. They may seem vast sprawling areas of poverty and overcrowding, but they have also proved to be places of invention, economic activity, and new social connections. Informal urban settlements are on the rise and slum-dwellers and civic authorities can work together to create safe, vibrant places in which people can thrive. Sociology can help this process by providing observations and analysis of the experiences of the people living there.

See also: 56–57

RURAL LIFE

URBAN LIFE

LIVING IN THE COUNTRYSIDE MAY MEAN BEING PART OF A COMMUNITY WITH SHARED VALUES AND STRONG BONDS—A STATE KNOWN AS GEMEINSCHAFT.

CITY LIFE CAN MEAN THAT RELATIONSHIPS ARE MORE FUNCTIONAL AND ANONYMOUS—A STATE KNOWN AS GESELLSCHAFT.

TRADITIONALLY, RURAL LIFE WAS LESS LONELY THAN URBAN LIFE

A sense of COMMUNITY

WHEN THE SUBJECT OF COMMUNITY COMES UP IN CONVERSATION, IT BRINGS TO MIND A GROUP OF PEOPLE WHO KNOW EACH OTHER WELL AND PROBABLY LIVE IN THE SAME AREA. TODAY, HOWEVER, THERE ARE COMMUNITIES OF PEOPLE THAT SHARE SIMILAR INTERESTS BUT HAVE NEVER MET EACH OTHER—EXCEPT VIRTUALLY.

What do we mean by community?

The concept of community evokes an image of a group of people who share a common culture and set of values, and, most importantly of all, live in the same area. This is the form of community featured in the key sociological study *Middletown: A study in contemporary American culture* (which was actually based on Muncie, Indiana) carried out in the 1920s by Robert and Helen Lynd. The study examined the habits and views of the inhabitants, what they aspired to, and how they passed their leisure time.

In the UK, Ray Pahl's influential 1970s work on the Isle of Sheppey, Kent, examined the nature of work in a small community. His study revealed how work is shared and how communities support an informal economy as well as more visible businesses. Both of these comprehensive studies shaped how sociologists came to understand communities.

Other types of community

Examining the subject more widely reveals that the term community can refer to other groups of people who may not be in the same physical place but who nonetheless stay in touch with each other. For example, we can talk about communities such as the gay community, the business community, or the student community, where a shared characteristic forms the basis for people's association rather than that they live in the same place. In an online community, by contrast, physical space is nonexistent and individuals connect via the internet.

There are 25 active virtual communities that have more than 100 million users.

See also: 50–51, 126–127

NO MAN IS AN ISLAND ...EVERY MAN IS A PIECE OF THE CONTINENT, A PART OF THE MAIN.
JOHN DONNE, ENGLISH RENAISSANCE POET AND ESSAYIST

A COMMUNITY KEEPS PEOPLE HEALTHY AND HAPPY

⊙ A social life

Living as part of a community can bring a variety of benefits through local involvement. However, attendance of many organizations is declining and we are even socializing less.

See also: 130–131, 142–143

Social capital

US sociologist Robert Putnam in his book *Bowling Alone*, published in 2000, argued that in the US there has been a decline in community involvement, with people being less likely to belong to any form of social group, and even choosing to go bowling alone. He blames television, women going out to work, a greater sense of individualism, the increasing amount of time spent at work, and de-industrialization for contributing to community decline.

Central to his thinking is the concept of "social capital." Usually, the word capital is associated with money (as in capitalism), but what Putnam is talking about here is a wealth of social connections. Various elements build social capital, but a key component is reciprocity, where people will pay back favors that others have done for them with other good deeds. These favors can range from looking after someone else's children, helping to shovel snow in winter, or other ways of being a good neighbor. Research has found that social capital is good for people's health, happiness, and safety, because they are more likely to be active and have people checking in on them.

Consequently, though, people may spend more time on their own these days, and a sense of community can help to maintain people's health and well-being.

THE ROSETO EFFECT

In the middle of the 20th century the town of Roseto, in Pennsylvania, was found to have below average levels of heart disease. Despite a diet high in fat and high numbers of smokers, it was a close community. This meant that no one was lonely and people helped each other deal with the stresses of life, which gave people a health advantage, known as the "Roseto Effect."

MAX WEBER

1864–1920

Max Weber was the eldest of seven children born into a German middle-class, intellectual family. Widely regarded as a brilliant student, he studied law, history, philosophy, and economics before becoming a professor of economics at the University of Berlin. Regarded as one of the founders of modern sociology, he is best known for his ideas on the role of religion in the rise of capitalism. Weber died at the age of 56, while working on his multivolume work *Economics and Society*.

A TROUBLED LIFE

Weber married Marianne Schnitger, a sociologist and feminist writer in 1893. Unfortunately, in 1897, he had a quarrel with his father that was never resolved. Following the death of his father shortly afterward, Weber suffered a nervous breakdown, which left him unable to work for five years. Weber's struggle with mental illness was described by Marianne in her influential biography of her husband, published in 1926.

> "The **fate** of our times is characterized... above all... by the **disenchantment** of the world."

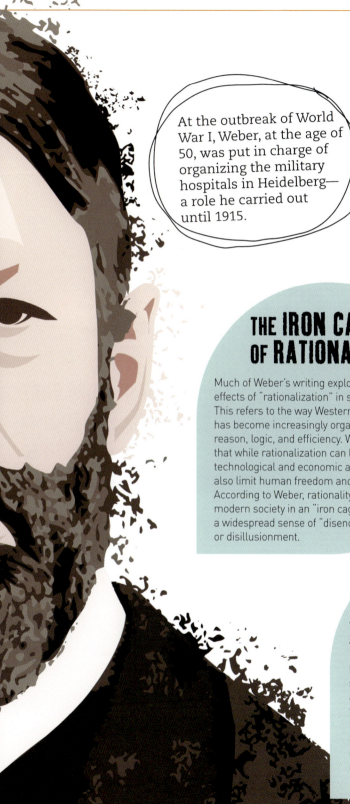

At the outbreak of World War I, Weber, at the age of 50, was put in charge of organizing the military hospitals in Heidelberg—a role he carried out until 1915.

THE PROTESTANT WORK ETHIC

Weber's most influential and controversial work, *The Protestant Ethic and the Spirit of Capitalism*, published in 1905, examines the relationship between Protestant beliefs and values and the rise of capitalism in the West. Weber claimed that although the Protestant values of self-discipline and hard work lay at the heart of capitalist societies, these religious ideals had been replaced by the relentless pursuit of profit and wealth.

THE IRON CAGE OF RATIONALITY

Much of Weber's writing explores the effects of "rationalization" in society. This refers to the way Western society has become increasingly organized around reason, logic, and efficiency. Weber argues that while rationalization can lead to greater technological and economic advances, it can also limit human freedom and creativity. According to Weber, rationality has trapped modern society in an "iron cage," leading to a widespread sense of "disenchantment" or disillusionment.

METHODOLOGICAL INDIVIDUALISM

Throughout his work, Weber adopted a method of analysis known as "methodological individualism." He believed that any study of social change should focus not on social structures, such as ethnicity or class, but on individuals and their actions. Weber was particularly interested in analyzing the motives behind human actions and the ways in which individuals in society interact and make sense of one another.

CONSTRUCTION WORKER

FARMER

STUDENT

CHEF

⬆ **Just the job**
Although earning money is very important, work also brings self-esteem, and gives us a purpose and status in society. It is also a place to build friendships and feel part of a team.

Why do we

WORK IS A MAJOR PART OF PEOPLE'S LIVES. WE SPEND MOST OF OUR WAKING HOURS AT WORK. SINCE IT TAKES UP SO MUCH TIME, WHY DO WE DO IT? OF COURSE IT IS TO EARN MONEY, BUT RESEARCH SHOWS THAT FINANCIAL GAIN IS ONLY PART OF OUR MOTIVATION.

> FAR AND AWAY **THE BEST PRIZE THAT LIFE HAS TO OFFER** IS THE CHANCE TO WORK HARD AT **WORK WORTH DOING.**
>
> THEODORE ROOSEVELT, FORMER US PRESIDENT

Not just about the money

In the US, the average employee between the ages of 25 and 64, who has children, will spend 8.9 hours a day at work, compared to 7.7 hours sleeping and 1.2 hours caring for others. Since work takes up so much time, it prompts the question, why do we do it? After all, for many people work can be a source of stress and drudgery. Now, the obvious answer is that work equals money, a weekly wage or an annual salary that pays for our rent or mortgage as well as other bills. But that is only part of the explanation.

First of all, the term "work" needs to be treated with caution. It is easy to think that work refers exclusively to paid work, something that is done in return for a wage, but there are many other forms of work, too. For example, for women, a major part of their time is spent doing domestic or caregiving work, which is often unpaid.

British sociologist Keith Grint explains that if you look across time and cultures it becomes clear that Western ideas of work are quite specific to that part of the world. For example, a work day stretching from 9am–5pm is not universal; in West Africa work is more attuned to the natural rhythms of the body, so you work when you feel awake and rest when you feel tired. Countries such as Spain and Greece used to have a work day that allowed for a rest, known as a siesta, during the hottest part of the day.

Work brings status

People are motivated to work for reasons other than money. Work can be a source of status, giving us a value in the world. Think about how common it is when first meeting someone to ask what they do for a living and how that then affects what you talk about

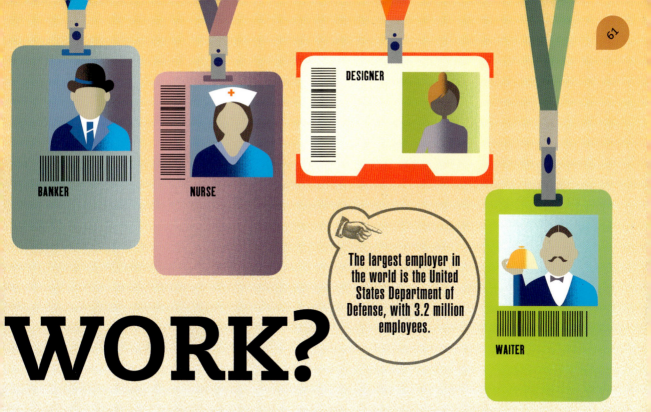

The largest employer in the world is the United States Department of Defense, with 3.2 million employees.

WORK?

next. Work is a place where people meet others and establish friendships that can last for many years. Work also provides structure in people's lives and provides a familiar routine. That is why many people find retirement or unemployment difficult, when they suddenly find they have so much time on their hands.

The work ethic

There are other deeper reasons for why people work. There is often a strong belief that work is a good thing, that it is one's moral duty to work, referred to as the "work ethic." German sociologist Max Weber, in trying to determine the roots of capitalist society in the West, saw that Calvinist Protestantism, the dominant religion in Germany at the time, played an important part in building this belief. Followers of the religion believed that God had already chosen who was going to heaven. Working hard and being successful on earth was a good sign that a person had been chosen. Hard work became part of the beliefs and practices of the faith. Over time the moral value of hard work has become separated from its religious roots but the practice has remained in the culture.

Expanding on this theme, sociologist Karl Marx believed that humans both want and need to work, and possess an array of creative talents in order to

do so. However, he believed that the way in which capitalist society is organized means that the natural capacity and need to work is distorted. Rather than work being a way to improve one's life or to help society as a whole, it has become for the benefit of an elite. Marx describes this situation as "alienation" and proposed that work under capitalism leaves people feeling unhappy and unfulfilled.

The reasons why we work are complex and multifaceted, but they are definitely about much more than the money.

WORKERS' COOPERATIVE

The Mondragon Corporation in the Basque region of Spain is a highly successful global business with a total revenue of $14 million, but it is run in a different way from most workplaces. It is a workers' cooperative, which makes it a more equal place to work. Workers vote on decisions affecting the business and even select the managers, who are not paid more than five times the wage of the lowest-paid worker.

How is work CHANGING?

A "JOB FOR LIFE" IS NOT A FAMILIAR CONCEPT TO TODAY'S HIGH SCHOOL AND COLLEGE GRADUATES. MOST YOUNG PEOPLE DO NOT CHOOSE TO FOLLOW A CAREER IN ONE PLACE. BUT HOW MANY EVEN HAVE THE OPTION? CHANGES IN MANAGEMENT STYLES AND THE JOB MARKET MEAN THAT THE WORLD OF WORK IS BECOMING LESS FULFILLING AND MORE UNSTABLE.

Secure jobs

The world of work is changing. Not that long ago, toward the end of the 20th century, people could expect to graduate from high school or college and, with perseverance and luck, find a job. Their work would give their lives structure, and possibly a career pathway leading to promotion. Stable employment was the foundation on which to build lifetime commitments such as raising children or buying a house. Work would also have provided a sense of self.

Soulless workplace

Today, work is less likely to guarantee long-term security and a predictable lifestyle, or be the same source of identity. There are many reasons for these changes, one of which is what sociologists call "new managerialism," the micromanaging of every aspect of the working day.

The research of British sociologists Phil Taylor and Vaughan Ellis on a call center is a typical example. The employees there had a tight script to follow. How well they stuck to it and how fast they worked was closely monitored. Deviation from the script or a falling-off in number of calls meant trouble.

To US sociologist Richard Sennett, a controlled workplace like this is a soul-destroying place to be. He says that work was once like a village, where people got things done but also had scope to make friends and feel part of a community.

See also: 60–61

Experts predict that by 2025 automation could take over 20–35 percent of current jobs.

IS JOB SECURITY A THING OF THE PAST?

On a tightrope
In today's precarious job market, many young people are forced to move from one type of short-term work to another. Opportunities for secure employment are rare.

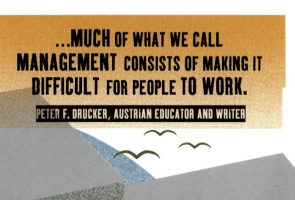

...MUCH OF WHAT WE CALL MANAGEMENT CONSISTS OF MAKING IT DIFFICULT FOR PEOPLE TO WORK.

PETER F. DRUCKER, AUSTRIAN EDUCATOR AND WRITER

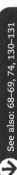

Now work is often more like a train station: you show up, do what is required of you, and go home again. It all lacks meaning.

The "precariat"

Another change in work is the rise in the number of people without regular full-time employment, who use online marketplaces to find jobs as and when available. The workers in this new economy are part of what British sociologist and economist Guy Standing calls the "precariat" in his book of the same name, published in 2011. The term is a fusion of the words "precarious" (insecure) and "proletariat" (working people). Standing points out how a younger generation is growing up knowing that they may never find a job to support the lifestyle they want. It is not, he argues, lack of will or skill that denies them opportunities, but how the current job market is structured.

Arrival of the robots

The final big change in the workplace is the development of automation. For example, many production-line tasks in the car industry have been taken over by machines. We do not know what will happen in the future. The list of jobs that could be automated is increasing. Office work and even doctors could be replaced by software or robots. What should be done for a workforce displaced by robots and automated systems will be one of global society's big challenges in the next few decades.

See also: 68–69, 74, 130–131

BETTY THE ROBOT
In the summer of 2016, a mobility systems company in the UK took on a trainee office manager: Betty the Robot. Betty, created by an international team at the UK's University of Birmingham, is a multitasker. Her artificial intelligence software enables her to assess staff presence, monitor the environment, check security, and meet and greet at reception.

ARLIE R. HOCHSCHILD

1940–

Arlie Russell Hochschild is a leading feminist and sociologist in the US. She studied sociology at Swarthmore College, then continued her studies at the University of California, Berkeley where she became interested in the role of emotions in sociology. In one of her most famous books, *The Second Shift* (1989), Hochschild discusses the roles and responsibilities women have at home and in the workplace. Her most recent work focuses on the relationship between emotion and politics in modern US society.

FEELING RULES

Hochschild was born in Boston, the daughter of US diplomats. As a child, she was fascinated by the way diplomats controlled their emotions in public. Later, she became interested in the way people are expected to feel certain emotions in given situations. For example, people are expected to feel happy when they get married or achieve good grades. Society, Hochschild claims, has distinct "feeling rules" that govern the way we manage our emotions.

EMOTIONAL LABOR

In her book *The Managed Heart* (1983), Hochschild introduced her theories on "emotional labor." This refers to the way employees are required to display certain emotions at work. Hochschild's research focused on a study of flight attendants in the 1980s, who were trained to behave as if they genuinely cared for their passengers. Hochschild claimed that this had a negative impact on the airline staff because, over time, they felt as if they had lost ownership of their own emotions.

"Most **women** work one **shift** in the office or factory and a '**second shift**' at home."

SERVICE WITH A SMILE

Much of Hochschild's research focuses on the role of women in the workplace. She claims that women are much more likely than men to work as store clerks, receptionists, or call center operators—jobs that require "good service" and high levels of emotional labor. Hochschild argues that this leads to gender inequality because it reinforces the idea that certain occupations are more suited to women.

In 1974, when her son was three years old, Hochschild wrote a children's book titled *Coleen the Question Girl*, which tells the story of a girl who can't stop asking questions.

EMOTIONS AND POLITICS

In her book *Strangers in Their Own Land* (2016), Hochschild looks at the way people's emotions affect their political choices. Over a five-year period, she traveled to Louisiana to talk to white working-class voters who felt let down by the US government. She tried to understand why, in an area that has suffered major industrial pollution, people blamed the government rather than the industries that caused the damage.

WATCHING

MODERN TECHNOLOGY MAKES WORKING LIFE EASIER FOR MANY PEOPLE, BUT IT IS ALSO A POWERFUL AND WIDELY USED TOOL FOR CONTROL. MILLIONS OF EMPLOYEES NOW ACCEPT AS NORMAL THE WATCHFUL EYE OF A SURVEILLANCE CAMERA AND THE POSSIBILITY OF THEIR ELECTRONIC DATA BEING INVESTIGATED AT ANY TIME. SOCIOLOGISTS ARE QUESTIONING THIS EROSION OF FREEDOM IN THE WORKPLACE.

Technology takes control

The workplace has changed a great deal since the Industrial Revolution that began in late 18th-century Britain drove technological development forward. Innovations swept on through the first half of the 19th century—most notably with the first mechanized computer and the electric motor. Since then, scientists have continued to develop ever more sophisticated machines and computers capable of performing tasks in a few minutes that in the past took workers many hours.

US sociologist and Marxist Harry Braverman, writing in the 1960s, saw technological advancement as the beginning of the end of work for human beings. He imagined a world where people were set free to devote their energies and extra leisure time toward developing their natural creativity and skills. His vision remains a distant reality, but Braverman's work highlighted the fact that technologically sophisticated equipment released the majority of workers from dull and demoralizing work on mass production lines, or repetitive and time-consuming desk work. However, at the same time as reducing physical workloads, modern technology is imposing limits on people's freedom in a new and subtle way.

"Dataveillance"

In the last decade, sociologists of work have focused attention on the ways technology has been appropriated in the workplace to increase productivity and efficiency. Surveillance technologies such as CCTV cameras, computer login counters, computer monitoring software,

MONITORING EMAIL

British sociologist Kirstie Ball's 2010 study of workplace technology found that out of 294 US companies with over 100 on staff, more than a third employed people with the specific task of reading through staff emails in search of rule-breaking. Ball's thought-provoking work also found that over 75 percent of US companies monitor not just employees' emails, but also check which internet websites they visit.

the workers

> ## TECHNOLOGY MAKES IT POSSIBLE TO GAIN CONTROL OVER EVERYTHING, EXCEPT OVER TECHNOLOGY.
> **JOHN TUDOR, US ATHLETE**

and electronic "swipe cards" are all used to gather information about the activities of staff. Knowing that at any moment CCTV footage covering your actions and data spreadsheets detailing your productivity can be called up on a computer screen has the same effect as a supervisor looking over your shoulder. According to Australian sociologist Roger Clarke, such monitoring devices were used initially by only a few employers. Now, with decreasing costs and widespread availability, surveillance technology is part of the modern workplace. Workers are subject to "dataveillance"—Clarke's term for the monitoring of employees' activities using personal data systems. Such systems include tracking the amount of time homebased employees spend at their computers; how long office employees are at their desks; and their movements in the work environment throughout the day.

Dataveillance is widely used for such purposes as tracking criminals and investigating identity theft.

Are you really alone? ❷
Even if you are working alone in your office, surveillance devices could be watching your movements and reading your emails.

Invasion of privacy?
According to Clarke, whether or not employers draw directly on the information generated by dataveillance, a significant part of their power derives from employees' awareness of being under constant scrutiny.

This suggestion has led to debates about the extent to which employers have the right to try to control employees' lives outside of work. A particular concern is the increasing tendency of employers to check up on what their staff posts on Facebook and online social media. Some areas of your personal life may be no more private than your work life.

See also: 80–81, 144–145

YOU COULD BE UNDER SURVEILLANCE

WORK AS PAIN

In 1844, at the age of 26, Karl Marx writes a series of essays that are known as the "Economic and Historical Manuscripts." His ideas on what he called "alienation" are developed here. Marx believes humans gain satisfaction from work. However, the drive for profit in the workplace denies people that satisfaction, making work a miserable and harmful experience.

RELIGIOUS DUTY

In 1905, Max Weber publishes *The Protestant Work Ethic and The Spirit of Capitalism*. In this work, Weber tries to answer why capitalism emerged in the West. He claims that its roots lie in the Protestant religions of the 1500s, which purports that if you work hard and do well during your life, then God will save you after death.

Social institutions
IN CONTEXT

SOCIAL GLUE

In 1912, Émile Durkheim publishes *The Elementary Forms of the Religious Life*. In it, he lays out the idea that religion acts as glue that holds society together. It does this in two ways. First, it provides sets of rules and behavioral norms that work to maintain social order. Second, religious rituals provide an emotional situation that binds practitioners together.

Jane Jacobs publishes *The Death and Life of Great American Cities* in 1961. She explains that cities can be large, but require small blocks of buildings that are a mix of residencies and stores to allow the community to interact. She advocates letting the residents and users decide on their own urban planning.

THE LIVEABLE CITY

The UN-Habitat program estimates that by 2030, 3 billion people worldwide will be living in slums (or more correctly, informal settlements). Life in slums is highly contradictory—they can be places of dense poverty, poor health, and squalor, while also offering community, social solidarity, and innovation.

SLUM LIFE

EDUCATION

According to UNICEF, there are 59 million children who are of school age, but who are not in educational institutions. These children are mainly living in sub-Saharan Africa (the area south of the Sahara Desert) where long-term poverty, inequality, and social unrest undermine their chances of receiving an education.

Our lives are structured around many important social institutions, such as work, religion, and education. These are at the core of our lives, although they are constantly undergoing changes that impact us all. Where we live is also a key factor in our lives because it gives us a community, whether it is in the city or in the countryside.

PRECARIOUS WORK

Guy Standing introduces the idea of precarious living in his 2011 book *The Precariat: The New Dangerous Class*. He outlines how work has become much more insecure. Workers today lack the employment rights of previous generations, and there is no guarantee of regular hours or regular wages. As a result, life has become more precarious.

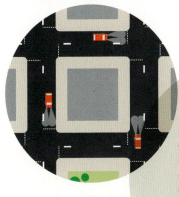

URBAN PLANET

In 2007, the world turns urban, meaning that now more than half the world's population lives in urban settings. Urban life offers exciting ways to live. New trends and ideas emerge in cities and people seek to make a new life for themselves. However, cities can also be lonely and isolating. It is easy to fall through the cracks and lose contact with other people.

When it all goes WRONG

WHY do people commit CRIMES?

BREAKING society's RULES

White-collar CRIME

Are we ALL on CAMERA?

WHODUNNIT?

HEALTH and EQUALITY

Not FITTING in

In any society, people have to face all kinds of problems and challenges, such as crime, physical or mental illness, and stress. Sociology helps us to understand the social factors that can make bad things happen. By studying particular groups of people, it is also possible to explain why life is harder for some members of a community than for others.

See also: 50-51, 126-127

Why do people

IT NEVER OCCURS TO MOST OF US TO TAKE UP A LIFE OF CRIME. HOWEVER, WHEN SOMEONE BREAKS THE LAW, PUBLIC FOCUS TENDS TO BE ON THE NATURE OF THE CRIME, NOT THE SOCIAL REASONS THAT MAY BE BEHIND WHY IT OCCURRED. TO THE GENERAL PUBLIC, CRIMINALS DO NOT SEEM TO HAVE THE MORAL CONSCIENCE THAT WE EXPECT OF OURSELVES AND OTHERS.

Social pressures

Sociologists find it just as important to understand the social factors behind crimes as it is to analyze the criminal mindset. This means they try to explain how society can sometimes be the cause of a person's turning to crime. Drawing on French sociologist Émile Durkheim's ideas about how cultural values strongly affect the way people think and act, US sociologist Robert Merton developed his Strain Theory in the 1940s. It highlights the similarities, rather than the differences, between honest people and criminals.

According to the theory, a lawbreaker's motives are often influenced by the expectations of the surrounding culture. For example, in many societies, financial success is an acceptable goal, but while most people make a profit lawfully, others make it through crime. Such criminals are likely to be motivated by the same socially legitimate ideals as the rest of us. They want security and an affluent lifestyle.

FOR SOME PEOPLE, CRIME TAKES THE PLACE OF WORK.

"Innovation"

Most people conform to approved moral standards to achieve security and a comfortable life. They get an education, find a job, and try to advance their status within the social structure. According to Merton, where disadvantaged and marginalized people have minimal chance of realizing such ideals, there is a greater likelihood that they will commit crimes.

Worldwide, theft is by far the most commonly committed crime.

Anyone living in an area of high unemployment, where access to education is limited, or ethnic and religious discrimination are widespread, could find it difficult to join mainstream society. When this happens, claims Merton, people face a choice. They must either accept life on the margins of society, or do what Merton calls "innovate": that is, use illegal means to gain legal ends.

commit **CRIMES**?

❂ Business world

Apart from the unlawfulness of their "work," some organized criminals can be compared to businessmen. More likely to carry a briefcase than a sack of loot, they follow their activities with an eye on market conditions.

EVERY SOCIETY GETS THE KIND OF CRIMINAL IT DESERVES.

ROBERT KENNEDY, US POLITICIAN

there is a ready-made market for their products. But if the market does not exist then they have to try and create one. In the case of drug dealing, this can involve encouraging people to try drugs until they become addicted and dependent on a continuing supply.

By highlighting the innovative nature of such criminal activity, Merton does not condone it. His point is that crime often occurs because the wider social system fails to provide everyone with an equal opportunity for playing a legitimate role in society. Taking this view, attempts to reduce crime should move away from examining the natures of the offenders themselves. Rather, we should focus more on the social reasons that cause people to turn to crime.

See also: 76–77, 78–79, 84–85 →

Criminals in context

Merton does not see criminals as completely different from law-abiding members of society. He thinks that certain types of criminal, such as drug dealers, for example, can be compared to entrepreneurs operating in the world of commerce. Like other business people, criminals identify and source products to sell to make money. This implies that

CRIME BOSS

Al Capone was a notorious criminal born in a New York City slum in 1899. By his twenties, he had established a vast empire founded on supplying alcohol to the public at a time when the sale of alcohol was banned throughout the US. At his trial in 1931, Capone claimed that, as any businessman, he was merely supplying what people wanted. He was sentenced to 11 years in prison.

ÉMILE DURKHEIM

1858–1917

Émile Durkheim was born in Épinal, France, into a devout Jewish family. He chose not to become a rabbi like his father, and went on to study philosophy at the École Normale Supérieure in Paris. In 1887, he started teaching France's first official sociology courses at the University of Bordeaux. Regarded as one of the founders of sociology, Durkheim is best known for his theories on the structure of society and his writings on religion, suicide, and education.

A LIVING ORGANISM

Durkheim is best known for his views on the structure of society. He saw society as a "living organism," with different organs performing different functions. According to Durkheim, a successful society—like a healthy body—is a system of connected parts that work together. If one part is damaged, the rest of society cannot function properly. This approach to sociology became known as "functionalism."

ANOMIE

Durkheim believed that society is held together by shared values and beliefs. In his book *The Division of Labor in Society* (1893), he argued that as society became more industrialized, people's jobs became more specialized, and shared experiences in the workplace became less common. Durkheim used the word "anomie" to describe the sense of despair individuals felt as they became increasingly isolated in society.

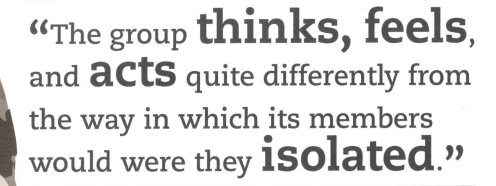

> "The group **thinks, feels,** and **acts** quite differently from the way in which its members would were they **isolated**."

SOCIAL FACTS

In his book *The Rules of Sociological Method* (1895), Durkheim argued that any study of society should be based on "social facts." These refer to institutions—such as religion, language, or education—that exist independently of people, but have power and control over their lives. Durkheim was interested in the way social facts hold society together and provide people with moral guidance.

After his only son, André, was killed during World War I, Durkheim's health declined rapidly, and he died in 1917, at age 59.

THE ROLE OF RELIGION

Although he turned away from Judaism as a young man, Durkheim strongly believed that religion had an important role to play in society. He argued that religious faith, especially long-established faiths such as Judaism, gave people a sense of belonging and community. In his work *Suicide* (1897), Durkheim noted that suicide rates were much lower in communities where people shared strong religious beliefs.

BREAKING society's

The oldest-known law code was written by a Sumerian king, Ur-Nammu, c.2100–2050 BCE.

IN ANY TYPE OF SOCIETY, WRONGDOING USUALLY INCURS PUNISHMENT. WE LEARN EARLY ON THAT BREAKING THE RULES, DEPENDING ON HOW SERIOUS THE CRIME, CAN LEAD TO ANYTHING FROM A PARENTAL ADMONITION TO A JAIL SENTENCE, AS WELL AS STRONG PUBLIC DISAPPROVAL. MOST OF US DON'T EVEN TAKE THE CHANCE.

See also: 74–75

Living by rules

We need rules. Without them, life would be unpredictable and unsafe. From childhood on, we learn that to be part of a group, such as a family, school, or workplace, we have to follow the rules. In some situations, such as knowing how to behave in public, we may need guidance from our parents. Often, however, we learn for ourselves what is acceptable behavior and what is not. Other rules are enforced by laws.

When people break rules, they are usually punished, but as society has changed over time, the nature of punishment has changed, too. According to leading British sociologist of crime and punishment David Garland, punishment is a "social institution." He means that it is created by people in a society and serves a range of functions, like any other institution.

WHEN **MORALS** ARE **SUFFICIENT, LAW** IS **UNNECESSARY...**
ÉMILE DURKHEIM, FRENCH SOCIOLOGIST

How we punish people

In his work *The Division of Labor in Society* (1893), French sociologist Émile Durkheim focused on how, over time, different forms of punishment have changed in line with an evolving society. In the past, people in organized communities were bound by what we call "mechanical solidarity": they were held together by common beliefs in certain values and standards of behavior.

REPAYING SOCIETY

In the US and UK, offenders convicted of certain crimes, such as drunk driving or underage drinking, can pay their debt to society by choosing to enroll in community-based programs. They might become involved in working with young people to warn them of the risks of using drugs, or help them improve their aspirations for the future.

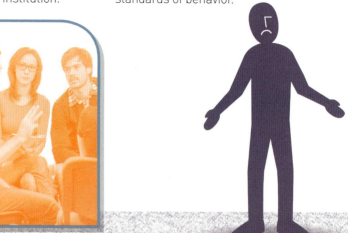

RULES

BEING NAMED AND SHAMED IS A DETERRENT TO CRIME

See also: 84–85

Good behavior
The dread of society's disapproval, and our own sense of what is right, keeps most of us on the right side of the law.

with a wrongdoer. In modern society, the job of punishing people falls to members of a designated social group, such as the police and the criminal justice system.

Fear of disapproval

Émile Durkheim believed it is not primarily fear of punishment that prevents most people from committing crimes. He suggested, rather, that people do not commit crimes because the moral values they absorb from society have a powerful restraining influence. We learn at a young age that breaking rules does more than risk punishment. Wrongdoing evokes guilt, embarrassment, and self-blame, especially if the culprit is caught. Thoughts of public exposure and family shame, and living with a guilty conscience, often prevent people from breaking the law in the first place.

Following on from Durkheim's ideas, David Garland notes that if prison numbers keep rising, it is not because the criminal justice system does not "work." It is because there are people who are too set apart from society to accept common codes of behavior or care about disapproval and accusations.

In such societies, lawbreaking caused outrage, and punishment was "repressive"; that is, the offender paid for the crime. A lawbreaker might be banished from the group or physically punished. By contrast, punishment in modern society is "restitutive." Instead of making lawbreakers outcasts or physically punishing them, today we aim at restoring them to society and repairing the damage they do.

Another difference, pointed out by German sociologist Norbert Elias, lies in who does the punishing. In much earlier ages, it was the victim, whether an individual or a community, who dealt

White-collar CRIME

NOT ALL SERIOUS CRIMES TAKE PLACE ON THE STREET. SOME OCCUR BEHIND THE RESPECTABLE DOORS OF MAJOR COMPANIES, HIDDEN IN COMPUTER FILES AND BURIED AMID COMPLEX DATA. THESE ARE SO-CALLED "WHITE-COLLAR CRIMES"—NONVIOLENT CRIMES COMMITTED BY PROFESSIONALS FOR FINANCIAL GAIN. SUCH CRIMES ARE HARD TO DETECT AND EXPENSIVE TO INVESTIGATE.

Corporate crime
White-collar crime is often connected to what is known as corporate crime. In such cases, an individual acts criminally on behalf of a company, rather than, say, with the aim of defrauding it.

TRANSFER OF FUNDS IN PROGRESS

Serious offenses
Some of the most serious offenses in our societies are "street crimes," such as murder, assault, and arson. These crimes typically receive a lot of public attention and have a huge impact on victims. Often, those on the receiving end of such violence do not hesitate to go to the police.

Just as serious, but less visible, are what sociologists call "white-collar crimes": misappropriation of funds, tax evasion, and fraudulent expense claims, among others. Although white-collar crimes may not cause physical injury, they do a lot of damage to people and businesses. Yet, often, no one reports them.

> I'VE FOUND MY EXPERIENCE IN THE **FINANCIAL WORLD** INVALUABLE BACKGROUND FOR WRITING ABOUT WHITE-COLLAR **CRIME.**
>
> SARA PARETSKY, AUTHOR OF DETECTIVE FICTION

See also: 74–75

Expert knowledge
Influential US sociologist Edwin Sutherland defines white-collar crimes as offenses committed by what he calls "persons of respectability" who are often at the top of their careers. Historically, white-collar crime has received far less attention from sociologists, the media, politicians, and law enforcement agencies than street crime. There

The majority of white-collar criminals are typically white, college-educated males.

are a number of reasons for this. Compared to property damage and violence, white-collar crime can be far harder to detect. Very often, expert knowledge is required to identify that a crime has taken place at all. Anyone attempting to bring legal action needs expert knowledge of complex tax laws in a case of fraud, financial regulations and laws in the case of insider trading on the stock market, and computer coding in the case of hacking and cybercrime.

Invisible theft
White-collar crime can be concealed and stay unnoticed for months or even years. A person can steal money by creating false expense claims that appear genuine unless closely

See also: 83–84

scrutinized. Small amounts of money can be "skimmed off" of business accounts. Unauthorized charges for services can be hidden among legitimate costs in a complex billing spreadsheet.

Even if white-collar crimes are detected, they often go unreported because bringing them out into the open can do further harm. Companies may not want to admit that they have been victims of theft, for fear that it could undermine the confidence of their customers. And admitting that a crime was carried out by "someone on the inside" may cast a shadow over the integrity of a company as a whole.

The true price of crime

US-based sociologist Joseph Martinez takes the view that white-collar crime is far less likely to be reported because many people think that, compared to violent crime, it is not such a serious offense. But white-collar crime comes at a high price. Research undertaken by US sociologist D. Stanley Eitzen shows that the average cost to the US government per street crime is $35. For white-collar crimes such as tax evasion, embezzlement, and fraud, the cost is a staggering $621,000.

Drawing on Eitzen's research, Martinez suggests that white-collar criminals should be subject to harsher punishments than street criminals because they cost society so much more. He believes that by handing out lesser punishments for white-collar crime than for street crime, law enforcement agencies appear to be trying to preserve social order at the expense of true justice.

CRIME IS SOMETIMES JUST A CLICK AWAY

BILLION DOLLAR FRAUD

Occasionally, a high-profile case brings the cost of white-collar crimes to public attention. In a notorious financial case of the 1990s, English-born trader Nick Leeson hid losses of $1.4 billion dollars from the Singapore financial trading company where he worked. Following police investigations, the company collapsed, leading to the layoff of hundreds of employees. Leeson was jailed for three and a half years.

Are we all on

It is now possible to buy tiny spy cameras that are small enough to hide in a shirt button.

WHEREVER WE GO IN PUBLIC PLACES, WE ARE PROBABLY ON CAMERA. SURVEILLANCE SYSTEMS TRACK US IN STORES, ON THE ROADS, AT AIRPORTS AND TRAIN STATIONS, ON BUSES, AND IN SUBWAYS. THESE SO-CALLED "SPY CAMERAS" ARE A PROVEN METHOD OF REDUCING BAD BEHAVIOR. BUT ARE THEY ALSO A HIDDEN FORM OF MIND CONTROL?

Our surveillance society

Big Brother is watching you! For many people, the catchphrase conjures up the worldwide reality television show in which a group of contestants sharing a house is filmed live every moment of the day. More famously, Big Brother is the all-seeing, and possibly nonexistent, leader of the totalitarian state depicted by British writer George Orwell in his classic novel *Nineteen Eighty-Four*. First published in 1949, Orwell's tale describes a future society, in the year 1984, in which people's every word and action is watched by an

CAMERA?

> ## THE MORE STRICTLY WE ARE WATCHED, THE BETTER WE BEHAVE.
>
> JEREMY BENTHAM, BRiTiSH SOCIAL REFORMER

all-seeing authority. According to French social theorist Michel Foucault, the surveillance society that Orwell chillingly predicted has become reality.

Controlling people

In his best-known work, *Discipline and Punish* (1975), Foucault highlights how as modern society developed and people moved from countryside to towns large communities in small urban centers soon became unruly populations. This threatened social order, and the use of physical control was ineffective.

To address the problem, 18th-century English social reformer Jeremy Bentham developed his theories on how to regulate society by controlling people's minds, rather than their behavior.

◉ On screen
The CCTV camera watches, but who, if anyone, is looking at the images it captures?

The Panopticon

Bentham's most influential idea was his design for a prison he called the Panopticon (from the Greek words *pan*, meaning "all," and *opticon*, meaning "to observe"). This is a ring-shaped prison, in the middle of which is a central watchtower. In the circular outer walls are numerous cells, each containing a prisoner. The prisoners cannot see whether or not there is a watchman inside the tower, so they never know when they are being observed. The constant uncertainty puts pressure on them to behave well at all times.

Power over the mind

Foucault sees Bentham's prison (which was never built) as a model for understanding the power of surveillance in today's society. The CCTV camera is the modern technological version of the Panopticon. Being under its eye creates uncertainty, and the vast majority of people react by assuming that they are permanently on camera and that someone is watching.

The more people become used to surveillance, the less they tend to take notice of it. But, often unconsciously, they are still conditioned to regulate their behavior. For Foucault, this is a good illustration of real power: It works by influencing people in ways they are not aware of. As a result, claims Foucault, people become less resistant to the effects of such power, because for much of the time they do not realize that they are being controlled.

See also: 48–49 →

WHODUNNIT?

CRIME BOTH HORRIFIES US AND GRIPS OUR IMAGINATION. SOMETIMES, THE WAY OFFENDERS ARE CAUGHT THROUGH A TINY SCRAP OF EVIDENCE SEEMS MORE LIKE CRIME FICTION THAN FACT. BUT MODERN LAW ENFORCEMENT AGENCIES HAVE DEVELOPED SOME HIGHLY SOPHISTICATED INVESTIGATIVE TOOLS, ONE OF WHICH IS CRIMINAL PROFILING.

Not just crime fiction

From Sherlock Holmes, supersleuth of Victorian London, to the myriad 21st-century popular television crime series, stories and films have planted the idea in our minds that by examining the nature of crimes, investigators can build up a profile of the criminal. While Holmes and television's crime scene teams are fictional, their methods are rooted in reality.

Serial offenders

Investigators first used criminal profiling to try to catch serial offenders, picking up the behavioral clues they left at the scenes of their crimes. Law enforcement agencies are most likely to seek the help of profilers in cases that are seemingly motiveless or when few clues are left at the scene of the crime. Similarly, when high-profile cases, such as a possible kidnapping, cause public alarm, police and profilers collaborate until the suspect is found.

Profiling tends not to be used for more "everyday" types of crime, such as burglary. In pursuing criminals, law enforcement agencies use profiling techniques developed in line with a range of studies, including sociology, psychology, and criminology (the scientific study of crime). The theory behind profiling is that, whether they know it or not, all offenders are shaped by certain social and psychological factors that criminal investigators use to construct the offender's identity.

See also: 34–35, 72–73

CRIMINAL PROFILING WAS PIONEERED IN THE LATE 1970S AT THE BEHAVIORAL SCIENCES UNIT OF THE FBI ACADEMY IN QUANTICO, VIRGINIA.

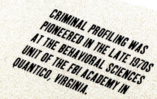

IT'S ALL IN THE DETAIL. CLUES AT A CRIME SCENE

THERE IS NOTHING LIKE FIRSTHAND EVIDENCE.

SHERLOCK HOLMES
(FROM *A STUDY IN SCARLET*, BY SIR ARTHUR CONAN DOYLE)

Creating a profile

Social structures such as gender, ethnicity, and social class are what shape people's patterns of acting and thinking. For example, class strongly influences the type of work people do. Gender and ethnicity contribute to the way a person lives and socially interacts. The job of criminal profilers is to identify the patterns in an offender's behavior. Drawing on sociological and psychological thinking and methodology, profilers make a key distinction when trying to catch serial offenders: is the suspect "organized"

CATCHING THE "UNABOMBER"

Between 1969 to 1995, Theodore Kaczynski, known as the "Unabomber," escaped detection by the US police for making and planting bombs. FBI profiler John Douglas deduced that the bomber was white, highly intelligent but underachieving, and either living alone or with someone who would not question his whereabouts. When Kaczynski was arrested in 1995, police discovered he had been a university professor who quit his career early and eventually lived as a recluse in a remote cabin in Montana.

2

3

CAN DEFINE THE NATURE OF THE CRIMINAL.

As well as having police experience, criminal profilers are usually trained in psychology and forensic science.

4

or "disorganized"? Organized offenders tend to lead well-regulated lives, a fact reflected in the relatively ordered and planned nature of their crimes. They are often of average to high intelligence, in a professional occupation, socially adept, and possibly married or in a relationship. Generally, organized serial killers commit murder in the period following a sudden destabilizing event, such as job loss, a relationship breakdown, or the death of a loved one. Because of their social status and capabilities, these offenders are likely to use their interpersonal skills to entrap their victim.

By contrast, disorganized offenders are often opportunists and their crimes are less likely to be premeditated. Many are unemployed, unsettled, socially inadequate, and unable to maintain personal relationships. They are also more likely to offend when under the influence of drugs or alcohol. Disorganized offenders tend to live relatively close to where they commit their crimes. The lack of planning characteristic of the wider life of a disorganized offender is mirrored in the signs of spur-of-the-moment chaos found at the crime scene.

See also: 84–85, 88–89

HOWARD BECKER

1928–

Howard Becker was born in Chicago. After studying sociology at the University of Chicago, he moved to Northwestern University, where he became a professor of sociology. He is best known for his "labeling theory," which questions why some types of behavior and individuals are regarded as "deviant," meaning outside the normal rules of society. A talented musician and jazz pianist, he is particularly interested in the role of art and artists in modern society.

> "**Deviant** behavior is behavior that people so **label**."

THE LABELING THEORY

In his book *The Outsiders* (1963), Becker examines why certain individuals and actions come to be labeled as criminal or "deviant." In Becker's view, there is no such thing as "deviant" behavior. An act only becomes deviant if powerful people in society, such as judges or politicians, label it as such. Becker argues that because those in power tend to be from middle or upper classes, they are more likely to negatively label people from a lower social class.

By the age of 15, Becker was working as a pianist in clubs in Chicago, where he witnessed firsthand how musicians came to be labeled as "outsiders" in society.

ON THE OUTSIDE

Becker was interested in the effects of labeling people as "outsiders." He believed that people who are labeled as deviant are more likely to behave in a deviant way in the future. For example, teenagers, who live in inner-city areas ruled by gangs, might be labeled as "gang members" even though they are not. Being labeled this way for long enough, however, may increase the chances of teenagers behaving like gang members to live up to the label.

SOLITARY ARTISTS

Becker disagreed with the view that artists—such as musicians, playwrights, and painters—work in isolation, outside "normal" society. In his book *Art Worlds* (1982), he points out that many specialists are needed to produce works of art. Artists rely on a wide network of people—including other artists, suppliers of materials, distributors, critics, gallery owners, and audiences—who together make up the art world.

MAKING IT CLEAR

Throughout his teaching career, Becker encouraged his students to explain their ideas in a clear and concise way. He was critical of the way some sociologists used complicated language to present their research. In his 1986 book *Writing for Social Scientists*, Becker offered students and academics practical advice on writing about sociology in a readable and engaging way.

See also: 24–25, 34–35

THE SOCIETY IN WHICH WE LIVE MAKES

HEALTH and

WE USUALLY THINK OF HEALTH IN TERMS OF WHAT WE DO WITH OUR BODIES: HOW OFTEN WE EXERCISE, WHAT WE EAT, AND HOW MUCH WE SMOKE OR DRINK. BUT THE SOCIAL GROUP TO WHICH WE BELONG AND THE DEGREE OF CONTROL WE HAVE OVER OUR LIVES AFFECT OUR WELL-BEING, TOO.

> BEING MARGINAL IN SOCIETY CAN INCREASE RISK... LIVING IN SUPPORTIVE... SOCIAL GROUPS CAN BE PROTECTIVE.
> MICHAEL MARMOT, WORLD HEALTH ORGANIZATION

Patterns of health

Food, drink, and exercise are definitely key parts of the health story but they do not make up the whole of it. The reasons for good or poor health are much more complex than that. The main part of the story lies with the kind of society in which we live and our place within it. If we examine health data, looking for patterns and trends, what we will find are differences among societies and among different groups of people within the same society. Typically, in countries with greater social equality, people tend to enjoy better health than those living in countries with less equality. People in the Nordic countries (Norway, Sweden, Iceland, and Finland), almost without exception, have the longest life expectancies in the world, longer than in the US or the UK. We can find the reason for such differences by looking at what it is like to live in those countries. In Nordic societies, with their greater emphasis on equality, there is a spirit of cooperation and looking out for each other. In the English-speaking countries, societies put the emphasis on competitive individualism, where the winners take all and the losers take, or are offered, very little.

See also: 88–89, 94–95

⊘ Set apart
Being seen negatively
because of social group
or ethnic origins can have
a damaging effect on
someone's health.

A SURPRISING DIFFERENCE TO OUR HEALTH.

equality

Human
life expectancy
varies enormously, from
around 50 years in the
poorer parts of the world to
well over 80 years in
more affluent nations.

Health and social status

There are also differences within a society, where life
expectancy and illness rates are determined by social
groupings. People lower down the social scale and
those who belong to ethnic minorities tend to have
poorer health. It is not simply the case that some
people choose, or cannot afford, to eat healthily or
that they get less exercise than they should. The
crucial issue is having the power and control to
make life worthwhile.

   Nearly everyone has choices of some kind, but we
do not all have access to the same resources that
allow us to decide what we want to do or be. Again,
this depends on the society in which we live. If you are
to be poor it is better to be poor in Norway than to be
poor in the US. Why? Because in Norway you will
have more resources—not just money but also in
terms of not being seen negatively, as poor people
can be seen in the US. You will therefore have
enough financial security and emotional strength
to lead a purposeful life.

Research into the
health of people of Black-
Caribbean heritage in the
United States and in England
provides another example of why national
context matters. Although these people share
a common ancestry and culture, they experience
life quite differently. In England, Black-Caribbeans
face more negative racist stereotyping than Black-
Caribbeans in the US. The result? The health of
Black-Caribbeans in England is worse than their
US counterparts.

Equality is good for health

So, while eating sensibly and getting regular
exercise are important, the more fundamental
influence on our health is our society. If everyone
lived on equal terms, enjoying equal opportunities
for shaping meaningful lives, then the overall
health of our societies would improve more than
if we all started jogging.

Not FITTING in

PROBLEMS WITH MENTAL HEALTH ARE INCREASINGLY COMMON IN OUR STRESSFUL WORLD. IN THE US, ONE IN FIVE PEOPLE WILL HAVE SOME SORT OF MENTAL HEALTH ISSUE DURING THEIR LIFE, AND AROUND 13 PERCENT OF 8–15 YEAR OLDS HAVE HAD A DIAGNOSABLE MENTAL DISORDER IN THE LAST YEAR. SOCIOLOGISTS BELIEVE THE MOST COMMON MENTAL HEALTH PROBLEMS, DEPRESSION AND ANXIETY, ARE RESPONSES TO LIVING IN OUR COMPLEX AND DEMANDING SOCIETY.

Getting a diagnosis

British sociologist Joan Busfield has identified a number of ways in which sociology can help us understand aspects of mental illness. She believes that a wide range of behavior has come to be considered "abnormal," when it could be an understandable reaction to life's difficulties. She also claims that doctors often prescribe medication because they lack specific training in dealing with mental health problems.

Unlike a physical illness, such as a tumor, you cannot use an X-ray to identify problems with someone's mental health. When someone is given a diagnosis of a mental illness by a health care professional, there is a possibility that social prejudices and stereotypes around gender, ethnicity, sexuality, and class may have affected what the patient said and how that was received by the health professional. For example, someone may describe their feelings by saying "I have a pain in my heart" or "I am feeling blue," but both of these phrases are metaphors and are open to different interpretations. It can be very hard to describe emotional difficulties and the words used will vary depending on the culture and social group to which the person belongs.

The effects of inequality

What sociological research reveals is that there are a number of social causes of mental illness in society. British researchers Richard Wilkinson and Kate Pickett, who specialize in the connections between society and health, discuss in their 2009 book *The Spirit Level* that mental health can be affected by income inequalities in a society. By this they mean that the greater the income inequality (the gap between the richest and the poorest in society) then the higher the level of mental illness. In societies where income is highly unequal, such as the US and the UK, there is

SUPPORT FROM FRIENDS AND FAMILY CAN HELP PEOPLE RECOVER.

WHY IS IT THAT **ANY OTHER ORGAN** OF YOUR BODY **CAN GET SICK AND YOU GET SYMPATHY...?**

RUBY WAX, COMEDIAN AND MENTAL HEALTH CAMPAIGNER

a tendency for individuals to be overcompetitive and dismissive of people who are struggling and appear not to have succeeded in life. These societies make impossible demands on people to show that they have a perfect life—one filled with the most sought-after consumer goods (such as smart phones, the right clothes, and so on), with the perfect, happy family and social life, too. This can feel like a lot of pressure.

As many as 11% of people in the US take an antidepressant daily.

The effects of stigma

Another problem faced by people with emotional distress is stigma. In his book, *Stigma* (1963), US sociologist Erving Goffman talks about how people work hard to maintain a front of normality, and avoid encountering negative reactions, if they have something they want to keep hidden, such as a mental illness. This requires exhaustive planning and leads to more psychological stress. More recently, in 2014, US sociologists Bruce Link and Jo Phelan also looked at research on mental illness and stigma. What they found is that people with a mental illness are discriminated against, and the realities of mental illness are poorly understood, which affects people's recovery. People with a mental illness may be seen as lazy, weak, or dangerous. They may be isolated from their friends and family, who are important forms of social support, and they may feel ashamed of their illness. All these negative attitudes create a false idea of what it is to be someone with a mental health issue.

GOING THROUGH A PERIOD OF DEPRESSION CAN FEEL ISOLATING AND STIGMATIZING.

MENTAL DISTRESS CAN BE A RESULT OF THE DEMANDS OF OUR COMPLEX AND COMPETITIVE SOCIETY.

⬆ Getting sick

When people suffer from depression or anxiety they can feel very isolated and stigmatized. Few people understand what having a mental illness is really like.

HEALTH WARNING

In his 2007 book *Affluenza* (a mix of the words affluence and influenza), British psychiatrist Oliver James found that the social pressure to acquire wealth is bad for mental health. He writes about Sam, who is a thirty-five-year-old New York stockbroker. Sam has a luxury apartment and a personal chef. But wealth does not make him happy; he leads an isolated life and finds it hard to form deep relationships.

MENTAL HEALTH

As far back as the ancient Greeks (around 480 BCE), there was an awareness of depression, which they called melancholia. In the 10th century, Persian scholar Al-Akhawayn Bukhari described a variety of mental health issues. He advocated the eating of certain foods and produced his own recipes, using plants and herbs, to help sufferers.

ANOMIE

Anomie, an important concept in sociology, is associated with French sociologist Émile Durkheim and his 1897 book *Suicide*. Anomie is the idea that some people are adrift from the rest of society or alienated from it. The way work, in particular, is organized means that individuals struggle to find meaning in what they do.

Crime and health
IN CONTEXT

DEVIANCE

In 1895, Émile Durkheim introduced the idea of deviance to sociology. His observation was that deviance is relative and relies on context. For example, until the 1960s, same-sex relationships were illegal and considered deviant in the US and UK, while some South American countries had legalized homosexuality in 1831 (Brazil) and 1887 (Argentina).

HEALTH

It was Talcott Parsons' identification of the "Sick Role" in 1951 that opened up the study of health for sociology. He introduced the idea that being sick is a role with four social expectations: being exempt from normal duties; not being responsible for being sick; wanting to get better; and seeking help and cooperating in trying to get better.

RACIAL **TENSION**

One sign of racial tension in the US is the number of young black men who have died as a result of police action. According to the *Washington Post*, 963 people were killed by the police in the US in 2016, and 41% of these were black or Latino, although they make up only 31% of the US population. Of those who were unarmed, 33% were black men, although they are only 6% of the US population.

MEDICALIZATION

One trend in health is what sociologists call "medicalization," where everyday problems that were once thought of as troubling but normal now come under the control of the medical professions. In British sociologist Susie Scott's 2007 book, *Shyness and Society*, she describes how conditions such as shyness are now seen not as a personality trait, but as something that requires medication.

Sometimes things go wrong in our society: people may behave in ways that seem to be out of step with the rest of society and be labeled deviant or a criminal. What sociology shows is that it is not always the individual who has a problem—sometimes society itself needs to change and see things differently.

BROKEN WINDOWS THEORY

In 1982, US researchers James Wilson and George Kelling offered the Broken Windows Theory, which states that if the police let minor crimes go unpunished (such as breaking windows), then this will lead to more serious crimes. Also called zero-tolerance policing, the theory informed police strategy in New York in the 1980s, when police targeted graffiti on subway trains.

SURVEILLANCE

We are used to living in a world surrounded by cameras that trace and track what we do. French philosopher Michel Foucault's book, *Discipline and Punish* (1975), was one of the first to spot this trend. He wrote about how surveillance "tricks" people into good behavior by making them think they are being watched when there is little chance that they are.

Why is the world so UNFAIR?

SuperRICH!

WEALTH and STATUS

The POVERTY trap

Who's to BLAME?

WHERE did RACISM come from?

Why haven't developing countries DEVELOPED yet?

Is GLOBALIZATION a GOOD thing?

GLOCALIZATION

What's our IMPACT on the PLANET?

Many sociologists have studied the reasons for the inequalities in our world, and why some countries are much wealthier and more successful than others. The answers may lie in the global economy and the way multinational businesses operate. Globalization of trade and industry has boosted opportunities for work worldwide, but does not benefit all nations equally in terms of money and status.

See also: 34–35, 62–63, 86–87

Super**RICH!**

BEING RICH IS NOT WHAT IT USED TO BE. THERE ARE MORE MILLIONAIRES AROUND THE GLOBE THAN THERE HAVE EVER BEEN. HOWEVER, THERE IS ALSO A NEW TYPE OF WEALTH THAT IS DESCRIBED AS "SUPERRICH," WITH A FORTUNE MEASURED IN BILLIONS RATHER THAN MILLIONS. HOW DID THESE PEOPLE BECOME SO INCREDIBLY WEALTHY?

World's richest people

In 2016, there were estimated to be 4,458,000 millionaires in the US. Being a millionaire in today's world is much more common than it used to be. In a report on inequality published in 2014, the charity Oxfam found that the wealth of the one percent of the population who are the richest in the world amounts to $100 trillion.

If we look at some of the most wealthy individuals, according to *Forbes* magazine, we find people such as Amancio Ortega, the Spanish owner of the clothing store Zara, with a personal net worth of $67 billion, or Warren Buffett, the US financier, whose net worth comes in at just over $60 billion, alongside Jim Walton of Wal-Mart, the US supermarket chain, who has a net worth of $33.6 billion.

It can be difficult to grasp what that sort of wealth actually means since the numbers are so huge. It might help to think hypothetically about weekly lottery winnings in the US. If the average weekly winnings are $18 million ($18,000,000), imagine that Bill Gates—with a net worth of $84.8 billion ($84,800,000,000)—won it. This would be the equivalent of someone with $84,800 winning $18.

Oxfam found that 8 individuals own the same as half of the world's population.

BILLIONAIRES

THE SUPERRICH ONE PERCENT OF THE POPULATION HAVE RICHES OF MORE THAN $100 TRILLION

Becoming superrich

How does this super-wealth come about? French economist Thomas Piketty wrote in 2014 that this super-wealth is not earned, in the way that you might imagine an entrepreneur creating a business from scratch. Rather, it is frequently inherited. Jim Walton and his family in the US are an example of that trend, inheriting their wealth from previous generations.

> **WEALTH IS NOW ITSELF INTRINSICALLY HONORABLE AND CONFERS HONOR ON ITS POSSESSOR.**
>
> **THORSTEIN VEBLEN, US ECONOMIST AND SOCIOLOGIST**

An exception would be the various tech giants who can become super-wealthy overnight, like Mark Zuckerberg of Facebook, who now has a net worth of $44.6 billion. So unless you are born into or marry someone from a rich family, or are a tech genius, then entering the world of the super-wealthy is challenging to say the least.

Wealth brings wealth

British sociologist Andrew Sayer's 2014 book, *Why We Can't Afford the Rich*, has also taken an interest in this super-wealth. He makes the point that a great deal of this money is also earned through financial deals such as the selling of stocks and shares. It is, he suggests, time to stop using misleading verbs such as "earned" when discussing the wealth of the superrich, because their existing fortunes get bigger just by accruing interest—without the rich having to do any actual work.

French sociologist Löic Waquant has also tried to understand inequality. He highlights how government policies in many advanced technological countries have favored the very wealthy—including cutting the tax they pay.

So, overall, being superrich today means belonging to a very small group. Perhaps questions have to be asked about how useful it is to have a few very wealthy people in society while so many more struggle to make a living.

See also: 96–97, 100–101

STRUGGLING TO LIVE

In the late 1990s, journalist Barbara Ehrenreich went undercover in the US working for minimum wage to explore the lives of low-wage earners. In her book, *Nickel and Dimed*, she writes about how life for these workers is very insecure—people live from paycheck to paycheck and work all the hours they can find, usually at more than one job. This has severe effects on their health and family life.

Excessive wealth
The lifestyles of the superrich are leaving the rest of us further and further behind. Inequality is increasing around the world meaning that a larger amount of wealth is held by fewer and fewer people.

Wealth and

SOCIAL STATUS CAN COME FROM BEING SUCCESSFUL AND BECOMING WEALTHY. SOMETIMES THIS SUCCESS COMES FROM HARD WORK AND TALENT, AND SOMETIMES IT COMES FROM INHERITED WEALTH OR FROM BEING FAMOUS FOR BEING FAMOUS. STATUS MATTERS THOUGH, AND MANY OF US TRY TO COPY WHAT THOSE WITH HIGH STATUS DO OR WEAR.

> Luxury items that become more desirable as their price goes up are known as "Veblen goods."

Gaining status

In our society, individuals such as sports stars, singers, and actors have wealth and status. Status refers to the standing and prestige in society that often stem from wealth and power but can also be gained by other means, such as by achievement. Other people such as prime ministers or presidents and writers have status for their achievements and influence, although they may not be especially wealthy. It is debatable whether today's celebrity sports stars and performers produce anything that benefits society; some would say they provide entertainment and inspiration, others that they contribute very little. Consequently, status can come from success—it does not have to come from producing something that significantly helps society.

Conspicuous consumption

In the late 19th century, US sociologist Thorstein Veblen wrote about the new consumer society he saw developing around him. He noticed how people were beginning to use consumer goods to draw attention to themselves in order to show off that they were better and wealthier than others.

In Veblen's book, *The Theory of the Leisure Class*, published in 1899, he outlined his idea of "conspicuous consumption." This important theory explored how a new social class, the business class, who had earned their money by setting up factories

> INDIVIDUALS... SEEK TO... GAIN THE **ESTEEM** AND **ENVY** OF FELLOW-MEN.
>
> THORSTEIN VEBLEN, US ECONOMIST AND SOCIOLOGIST

during the Industrial Revolution, spent their money as a way to display their status and how that in turn influenced other people below them in society.

In the 1800s, the wealthy tended to demonstrate their status by spending long periods in the countryside, traveling to foreign countries, or by not doing much at all. They were the "leisure class" who did not need to work. The new business class lived and worked in towns and did not have the same time to devote to leisure as the landed gentry. They needed another way to display their status,

STATUS

wealth, and power, and they achieved this by spending on lavish goods, in particular, clothing that was neither practical nor essential, but served instead to symbolize their success.

Of critical importance to Veblen was the impact of this process on people lower down the social scale. He saw that people were influenced by the actions of the business class. People who were poorer and less successful than the business owners tried to copy what the business class bought; they hoped by buying the same consumer goods and mimicking their wealthier peers they could raise their own status, sort of like saying, "Look at me, I am the same as the best people in society!"

Service to others

Another sociologist who looked at this subject was the German Max Weber. He agreed that money and power were important in building an individual's status in society but he also

SLIDING STATUS

Status can also work the other way around. There are groups of people in society who have money and power but do not have the social status to match. A consequence of the 2009 economic crash and subsequent recession was that the social status of bankers fell. Rather than being seen as the trustworthy custodians of people's savings, they were criticized for being greedy and incompetent.

See also: 100–101, 119

observed that people who were not rich could achieve high social status. For example, religious leaders, such as ministers or priests, are not well paid but command the respect of their community because they perform a job that involves self-sacrifice and service to others.

Copy cats

Those further down the social scale seek to copy the style adopted by the wealthy and successful in society, even they may not be able to afford to buy exactly the same item.

The POVERTY

Out of a global population of more than 7 billion, an estimated 3 billion people live at some level of poverty.

NOWHERE IN THE WORLD IS FREE FROM POVERTY. SOME SOCIETIES HAVE THE MEANS TO IMPROVE CONDITIONS FOR THE POOR, WHILE OTHERS DO NOT. BUT EVEN IN THE WEALTHIER NATIONS, PEOPLE ARE TRAPPED IN POVERTY BECAUSE BARRIERS SUCH AS AGE, GENDER, AND SCARCITY OF WORK PREVENT THEIR UPWARD MOBILITY.

In the trap

The "poverty trap" is a frequently used term describing the situation of people who cannot, for whatever reason, escape from being poor. No matter how wealthy the world becomes, significant numbers of people live in hardship. Sociology recognizes two degrees of poverty: absolute and relative.

Absolute poverty

Where people struggle to obtain the basics of life such as food, clothing, and a roof over their heads, we speak of them as being in "absolute poverty." This condition is more commonly associated with what are called low-income and middle-income nations (previously described as developing nations) or in societies that have collapsed, perhaps because of war or political, environmental, or economic crises. The World Bank defines absolute poverty as living on less than $1.90 per day. By that measure, statistics produced in 2013 show that 10.7 percent of the world's population can be included in the category.

Relative poverty

The other category is "relative poverty." People have the basics of life: they have shelter, clothes, and food, but they live at standards considerably lower than would be expected in their society. This means that what counts as poverty differs from society to society.

For example, in high-income nations (which used to be called developing nations), relative poverty could mean that a person has some consumer goods, such as a television or a mobile phone, and is still seen as living in poverty.

trap

A change of attitude?

There is much debate on how to tackle poverty and how to free people from the poverty trap. One view, first popularized by US sociologist Charles Murray in the 1980s, focuses on the attitude of poor people. According to Murray, the poor supposedly like being on welfare benefits and have no inclination to work. So, the theory goes, to stop poverty we need to get poor people to change their thinking and stop being work-shy. US politician Paul Ryan echoed this view in 2012 when he said that the "safety net" of benefits in the United States was becoming a "hammock," in which people were happy to spend their time idling and doing nothing to escape their poverty.

No way out

Many commentators, however, believe the reasons for poverty lie in the way in which society is structured. What this means is that no matter what someone does and how hard he or she may try, it may simply not be possible for them to escape poverty. For example, a person could face barriers to getting a job because of age, ethnicity, or gender. Or it could be that the overall economy is performing so poorly that jobs are not available. One recent trend in the workplace has been an increase in unstable, low-paid work that does not bring in enough income to increase someone's overall standard of living. Sociologists continue to research the options for ending the vicious circle of poverty.

FINNISH EXPERIMENT

In 2017, a two-year trial project began in Finland to try to lift people out of poverty. Two thousand unemployed people randomly selected by the government receive a monthly income of €560 (around $650) instead of state benefits. Anything they earn on top of this they can keep without losing the basic income (whereas benefit would be cut) so even low-paid jobs make a difference.

See also: 100–101, 104–105

Caught in a net

Some countries have a benefits "safety net" to keep people from falling too far into poverty. This net has been variously described as a "hammock" for the idle, or a trap that is impossible to escape.

> WHEN IN **POVERTY**, PEOPLE USE THEIR SKILL TO **AVOID HUNGER**. THEY **CAN'T** USE IT FOR **PROGRESS**.
>
> HANS ROSLING, SWEDISH DOCTOR AND STATISTICIAN

Who's to **BLAME?**

WHOSE FAULT IS IT IF SOMEONE IS POOR? DOES THE FAULT LIE WITH THE INDIVIDUAL OR IS IT SOCIETY THAT IS TO BLAME? THIS IS AN IMPORTANT ISSUE FOR SOCIOLOGISTS. IT CHALLENGES IDEAS ABOUT PEOPLE'S CHOICES AND SOCIETY'S RESPONSIBILITIES. IT CAN MAKE US THINK ABOUT HOW MUCH CONTROL WE ACTUALLY HAVE OVER OUR LIVES.

Structure and agency

If someone is poor, should the blame for their situation rest with them or with society? This is a big issue in sociology and asks us to think about what sociologists call "structure" and "agency." Structure, or more accurately social structures, are the aspects of life that are beyond the control of an individual, such as the class into which a person is born, their gender, their sexuality, and their ethnicity. Agency (taking action) refers to the decisions that people make concerning their lives—what they choose to do.

From an agency perspective, the decisions, abilities, and the effort that someone puts into life is what shapes his or her circumstances. US sociologists Kingsley Davis and Wilbert Moore took that point of view in the 1940s. The two were interested in why certain people reached particular positions in society. For them, the answer was clear: people's position in life was the result of their abilities (intelligence, hard work, and other skills) and the choices that they made. The benefits of society (high income and social status) are therefore distributed to those who deserve them most.

INTELLIGENCE AND HARD WORK MAY NOT BE ENOUGH TO GET AHEAD IN LIFE.

See also: 36–37, 48–49, 94–95

KEEP YOUR COINS, I WANT CHANGE!

BANKSY, BRITISH ARTIST

Equal opportunities?

The majority of sociologists, however, see social structures, which are beyond the individual's control, as responsible for where people end up in life. They would say that the idea of agency assumes that everyone has access to the same opportunities and resources, and therefore any difference in outcome is determined by the choices individuals make. That, however, is far from the case. People have radically different access to opportunities and resources. The differences in opportunity depend on where someone is located in the structure of society. When society is analyzed, certain patterns appear again and again: individuals from minority or disadvantaged groups are blocked and frustrated in their attempts to get ahead in life.

SELECT SCHOOLS
Studies show that many top executives at leading multinational companies are very likely to have graduated from one of an elite group of universities that are recognized worldwide. These include the Ivy League universities in the US, Oxford and Cambridge in the UK, and the HEC Paris in France.

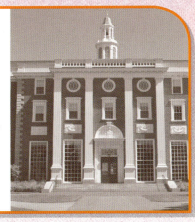

◉ Hard to move up
Sociologists disagree about whether people can break out of the social class into which they were born. Some believe hard work and talent will be enough, but many others think such opportunities are rare.

French sociologist Pierre Bourdieu identified one of the factors to blame for this unequal situation in society. In his work, he stressed the importance of what he called "social capital," or the valuable contacts that people have who could help them get a good job. People from affluent backgrounds are more likely to possess the social capital that will help them and their families do well in life. For example, the parents of a wealthy student who is not doing well at school may have a friend who runs a business, and who will help their son or daughter get a job. Further down the social scale, that kind of useful social capital is less likely to be found.

Useful connections
Studies have shown that some individuals have access to much better opportunities as a result of their family's social position. This means that a person born into a wealthy family has a much better chance of also becoming wealthy. It is also less likely for someone born into wealth, even if they do not do well academically, to slide into poverty.

The buying power of the average worker in the US has stagnated—it has not increased since 1979.

A bigger problem
One of the reasons why many people in modern society like to focus on an individual's responsibility for his or her success or failure is that this hides society's role in the process. Perhaps it is easier to blame the individual than it is to look at how people might be disadvantaged by the systems in society.

See also: 124–125, 126–127

Where did **RACISM**

THE DEVELOPMENT OF RACISM FOLLOWS ONE OF THE MOST BLOODY AND BARBARIC PATHWAYS IN HUMAN HISTORY. BELIEFS AND IDEAS BORN IN THE SLAVE-WORKED PLANTATIONS OF 18TH-CENTURY EUROPEAN COLONIALISTS REMAIN EMBEDDED IN SOCIETY TODAY. RACISM HAS CHANGED OVER TIME, BUT STILL AFFECTS THE LIVES OF MINORITY GROUPS IN MANY PARTS OF THE WORLD.

Looking at racism

The first African–American to gain a PhD. at Harvard University, sociologist W. E. B. Du Bois, made the observation in 1897 that black people feel "...a two-ness—an American, a Negro; two souls, two thoughts, two unreconciled strivings; two warring ideals in one dark body." He was reflecting on African–Americans' experiences of racism and how it was to feel not fully part of society. Du Bois was also interested in how racism developed in the United States. Part of his studies looked at how the Atlantic Slave Trade was central to the creation of modern-day racism.

Colonial power

The historical and social origins of modern racism lie in the expansion of European colonialism and the emergence of capitalism in the 17th and 18th centuries. At that point, many European nations, typically the British, Spanish, Portuguese, and French, were expanding their empires, founding colonies as far apart as Africa and the Americas.

One of the reasons for this upswing in colonialism was the immense potential wealth to be made from the cultivation of sugar, tobacco, and cotton. But there was a problem for the expansionists: there were not enough

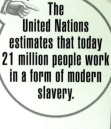
The United Nations estimates that today 21 million people work in a form of modern slavery.

SOCIETY IS NOT YET FREE FROM RACISM

◐ **Moving on**
We need to rid ourselves entirely of the shackles of racism, so that societies can move on and develop in better ways.

See also: 24–25, 26–27, 38, 91

come from?

people to work in the enormous plantations where the moneymaking crops were grown. The solution to this labor shortage was slavery.

Human cargo

The practice of owning people as property had existed for thousands of years. Slavery was common in ancient Rome and Babylonia, and long established in Africa, with Africans enslaving their fellow countrymen. But the slave trade of the 18th century was on a far vaster, industrial, and more brutal scale than anything ever known before. Around 12–15 million African people were forcibly shipped across the Atlantic. This was part of a system called the "triangular trade." Ships left England stocked with goods, such as rum and textiles, to trade with slavers in West Africa. They then sailed to the Americas, with a cargo of slaves who were treated as mere "goods," without human rights, and sold on arrival. The ships returned to England with cotton, sugar, and tobacco grown on the slave-worked plantations.

Inventing inequality

How could the slave traders morally justify themselves? In the early days, religious reasons had been used: Africans were not Christian, and therefore could be enslaved.

THOSE WHO **DENY FREEDOM** TO OTHERS, DESERVE IT NOT FOR THEMSELVES.

ABRAHAM LINCOLN, US PRESIDENT, 1859

But what if slaves became Christians, as many did? The more brutal justification arose, that black Africans were somehow inferior to white Europeans and so it was permissible to treat them without care or dignity. Such ideas, begun on the plantations, spread to Europe, where so-called scientists such as Frenchman Arthur de Gobineau in 1848 published work supposedly proving racial inequality.

Today, the idea of white superiority has largely (although not completely) vanished, to be replaced with something more subtle. British sociologist Paul Gilroy, in his studies of the 1980s, noted that modern racism was expressed not in biological terms but cultural terms. He also saw that society must stop regarding race as a way of identifying people.

See also: 104–105, 106–107

UNDERGROUND RAILROAD

On the plantations of the American south in the 19th century, slaves were seen as possessions, not people. Their only chance at freedom was to flee north. A secret network called the Underground Railroad helped enslaved people escape to freedom. It may have aided as many as 100,000 slaves. Harriet Tubman (right), a former slave herself, was the most famous of the Railroad's "conductors," who led people to safety.

Why haven't **DEVELOPING** countries developed yet?

WHY IS IT THAT SOME COUNTRIES ARE STILL NOT ABLE TO CATCH UP WITH THE DEVELOPED ECONOMIES OF THE US AND WESTERN EUROPE? SOCIOLOGIST IMMANUEL WALLERSTEIN BELIEVES THAT IT IS NOT BECAUSE THESE COUNTRIES ARE NOT CAPABLE OF SUCCEEDING BUT BECAUSE THERE IS A WORLD SYSTEM IN PLACE THAT DISCRIMINATES AGAINST THEM.

> The UN's Sustainable Development Goals target 2030 is for everyone to have decent education, health, well-being, and housing.

An unequal system

US sociologist Immanuel Wallerstein set out in his 1974 book *The Modern World System* a bold explanation for why some countries have not achieved the same level of development as others. His central claim is that the world is locked into a system that creates unequal—even exploitative—relationships between nations. It is not that the countries themselves are incapable of developing but rather that they are held back by an economic system that creates an unequal situation similar to a class system.

The origins of this unequal relationship lie in the colonial expansionism of European nations in the 16th century. This was when the nations of Europe, such as the Netherlands, France, and the UK, set up trading relationships with countries around the globe, using their superior ships and military might to their advantage. The inequality continues today with the spread of globalization, which benefits the most well-off countries at the expense of the poorer nations.

Three positions in the system

Wallerstein's theory puts countries into one of three positions. The most powerful countries form what he calls the "core" of the world system. These are highly

THE PERIPHERAL COUNTRIES ARE POOR. THEY ARE MAINLY AGRICULTURAL NATIONS, PROVIDING RAW MATERIALS AND CHEAP LABOR FOR OTHER COUNTRIES.

COUNTRIES IN THE SEMI-PERIPHERY HAVE INDUSTRY AND DEVELOPMENT. THEY MAY BE CORE COUNTRIES IN DECLINE OR HAVE ONCE BEEN PERIPHERAL NATIONS.

PERIPHERAL NATIONS

SEMI-PERIPHERAL NATIONS

developed technologically advanced countries, such as the US, Canada, and Japan. The core contrasts with the "periphery," which includes countries that are poor, less politically stable, lacking technological industries, and reliant on providing cheap labor. Finally, there is a middle ground of the "semi-periphery" for countries that sit somewhere between the core and periphery. They are definitely not rich but have escaped the poverty of peripheral nations. They can exercise some power, although not to the same extent as the core nations.

Not a fixed state

Wallerstein understands that the world is dynamic and countries can move between the various positions. It is therefore a matter of judgment where some countries can be placed in his theory. The US is easily at the core, as are the nations of Western Europe. At the turn of this century, China would have been placed at the periphery, but now it is in the semi-periphery and moving toward the core. Other nations including Brazil, Russia, and India have also developed rapidly over the last twenty years.

British sociologist Roland Robertson has made some criticisms of Wallerstein's theory. The focus on economics leads to a limited understanding of power, he says. Some countries can make an impact culturally and gain global prominence that way.

⊙ A world system
Countries occupy one of three positions according to Wallerstein's world system: they are either on the periphery, on the semi-periphery, or at the core.

See also: 102–103, 106–107, 108–111

CHINA RISING

Italian sociologist Giovanni Arrighi suggested in his 2007 book *Adam Smith in Beijing* that the US will slip further from its leading global role with the rise of China. This movement will not necessarily lead to China replacing the US, but instead create a world with several dominant economic, cultural, and military powers.

The small country of Iceland (population 250,000) is an example, where its music culture significantly raises its profile.

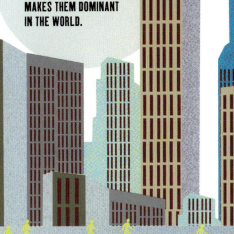

THE CORE COUNTRIES ARE WEALTHY. THEY EXCEL IN TECHNOLOGICAL INDUSTRIES AND HAVE A GREAT DEAL OF CAPITAL TO INVEST. THIS MAKES THEM DOMINANT IN THE WORLD.

CORE NATIONS

BOAVENTURA DE SOUSA SANTOS

1940–

Portuguese sociologist Boaventura de Sousa Santos is a professor of sociology at the University of Coimbra in Portugal and a visting professor at the University of Wisconsin-Madison. He is noted for his work on democracy, globalization, and human rights. He is particularly critical of the way Western society has dominated global social and political issues, while excluding the views of the world's poorest countries.

LIFE IN THE SLUMS

Born in Coimbra, Portugal, de Sousa Santos studied law at the University of Coimbra. While completing his postgraduate studies at Yale University, he developed an interest in sociology. As part of his fieldwork, he spent several months living in the slums (*favelas*) of Rio de Janeiro, Brazil. It was during this time that he became interested in the values and experiences of communities living in very deprived areas.

A DIVIDED WORLD

De Sousa Santos has written numerous books and articles on epistemology—the study of knowledge (taken from the Greek word *episteme* meaning "knowledge"). He suggests that the world is divided, not only by politics and economics, but also by knowledge and ideas. He argues that the richer, more developed regions of the "global North"—the northern part of the globe—have largely ignored the views and knowledge of the poorer "global South."

In 2001, de Sousa Santos founded The World Social Forum—an organization that promotes global economic and social justice.

"What cannot be **said**, or said clearly, in one **language** or **culture** may be said, and said clearly, in **another** language or culture."

MUTUAL RESPECT

Much of de Sousa Santos's writing focuses on the ways globalization has led to social inequality, government corruption, and environmental damage. Yet, in many countries where these problems are common, the ideas and experiences of local communities are overlooked. De Sousa Santos believes that global equality can only be achieved when there is "cognitive justice"—a term meaning mutual respect for different forms of knowledge.

AN ECOLOGY OF KNOWLEDGE

De Sousa Santos has campaigned widely for a global "ecology of knowledge," in which different countries share their knowledge and experience to deal with the problems of globalization. He argues that, for too long, the West has regarded its scientific knowledge as superior to all other types of knowledge. For an ecology of knowledge to truly flourish, the views and ideas of all cultures must have equal value and recognition.

Is **GLOBALIZATION** a good thing?

GLOBALIZATION IS THE PROCESS BY WHICH POLITICS, ECONOMICS, TRADE, INDUSTRY, CULTURES, AND COMMUNICATIONS INTERCONNECT AROUND THE WORLD. WHAT NO ONE COULD HAVE FORESEEN A FEW DECADES AGO IS HOW RAPIDLY THIS PROCESS WOULD PICK UP SPEED. SOCIOLOGISTS ARE TRYING TO EXPLAIN WHAT GLOBALIZATION COULD MEAN FOR US ALL.

The materials to make a pair of jeans may come from 10 or more countries.

Out of control

According to British sociologist Anthony Giddens, globalization is like a "runaway juggernaut." Once, the juggernaut's driver (human enterprise) was in control. But now the juggernaut (globalization) has gathered speed and a momentum of its own. The driver has lost control. The best anyone can hope for is that there is not a planet-sized catastrophe, such as irreversible environmental damage through over-industrialization .

Positive capitalism?

Economic theorist Immanuel Wallerstein is among those who believe that the unrelenting pursuit of profit has led to the spread of capitalism on a global scale. Crucially, when people in one country want to expand their businesses in other parts of the world, they are thinking not about globalization, but new markets and increased profit. Any local impact their business may have is largely unintended.

US sociologist Milton Friedman sees globalization positively. International and national capitalist trade will, he says, lead to better living standards, fairer distribution of wealth, and higher levels of material comfort for all. But not everyone agrees.

The power of TNCs

According to Polish sociologist Zygmunt Bauman, globalization, together with the spread of capitalism, does not lead to rising living standards for most people. It leads instead to greater financial insecurity, higher unemployment, and unhealthy competition. In Bauman's view, a key development in this state of affairs is the growth of transnational

GLOBALIZATION SHOWS NO SIGNS OF SLOWING DOWN.

ARGUING AGAINST GLOBALIZATION IS LIKE ARGUING AGAINST THE LAWS OF GRAVITY.

KOFI ANNAN, SECRETARY-GENERAL OF THE UN, 1997–2006

See also: 104–105, 110–111, 116–117

corporations (TNCs). These vast operations straddle the world, deciding where to build production plants, distribution points, and retail outlets in dozens of countries. The power of TNCs undermines the power of national governments to control their own economic and political fortunes.

"The space of flows"

The globalization of internet-based technologies is the focus of Spanish sociologist Manuel Castells. He calls the online world "the space of flows," a space in which people, goods, and information keep moving—

or flowing—around the globe. An ever-growing number of transactions takes place in the space of flows, including relationships via social media such as Facebook, blog sites, and dating websites, as well as online activities such as booking vacations, purchasing goods, e-banking, and so on.

At first, Castells saw the space of flows as something that worked only for elite groups wealthy enough to own internet-based technologies. But he acknowledges that the internet has now opened up to less privileged people. Ironically, these people see the space of flows as an important arena for raising awareness of, among other things, the damaging effects of globalization on the world's ecosystems.

FAIR TRADE

In the developing world, producers of goods for the global market often do not receive a fair price for their products or labor, or make enough profit to support their families. In the 1960s, the Fair Trade movement was pioneered with the goal of helping traders in poorer societies earn fair wages and improve their working standards. The "Fair Trade" label was first seen in the 1980s on coffee produced in Mexico.

◉ **Full tilt**
Globalization is beyond the control of any individual or nation. It is a powerful force that is reshaping the world, but sociologists do not agree on whether this is a good or a bad thing.

GLOCALIZATION

THE WAY NATIONS LINK UP AND TRADE WITH EACH OTHER (GLOBALIZATION) IS NOT JUST A TOPIC FOR ACADEMICS AND POLITICIANS TO TALK ABOUT; IT AFFECTS ALL OF US. SOME PEOPLE FEAR WE ARE IN DANGER OF LOSING NATIONAL DIVERSITY. BUT OTHERS BELIEVE THAT BY MIXING GLOBAL AND LOCAL VALUES, A PROCESS CALLED "GLOCALIZATION," WE CREATE NEW CULTURAL FORMS.

Making connections

The key to understanding globalization is what is called "connectivity." According to British sociologist Anthony Giddens, globalization is the increasing interconnection between different peoples and cultures. Giddens thinks that today we are communicating more often and within ever-widening networks. This closer connecting of people and

THINK GLOBALLY, ACT LOCALLY.

ANONYMOUS

nations, through the internet, budget air travel, and greater mobility, is largely seen as something positive. It leads to the freer flow of goods, services, and information. At the same time, however, there is growing concern about what globalization may be doing to the diversity of the world's cultures.

"Cultural imperialism"

Many people believe that globalization is diluting the ideas, values, and ways of life that make one human culture so distinct from another. Some sociologists take the Marxist-inspired view that sees globalization as "cultural imperialism." This term refers

to a process driven by powerful Western European and North American transnational corporations, or TNCs: for example, the giant media production companies, financial houses, and commercial organizations whose names are familiar in most parts of the globe. As these TNCs reach new markets, the local cultures with which they come into contact are taken over and brought into line with Western capitalist models. Whether we are in London, New York, or Beijing, we find the same brands of soft drinks or sports shoes close at hand.

A major US theme park replicated in Hong Kong was restructured to align with Chinese beliefs on harmony.

Global meets local

The work of British sociologist Roland Robertson challenges the idea that a crushing imperialist force is wiping out local individuality. He developed the term "glocalization" to demonstrate that, in reality, many people experience globalization as a mixture of "global" and "local" elements. Adapting global ideals and consumer goods to meet local needs and tastes can result in new goods and services tailor-made for a specific market.

See also: 104–105, 108–109, 118

IS THERE SUCH A THING AS A GLOBAL BURGER?

In Arab countries, for example, pita bread rather than buns is served in burger restaurants, along with spices that appeal to regional tastes. A major Western manufacturer of shaving razors has adapted its blades and fittings for use in an Asian market where water for shaving is scarce. Television series and soap operas devised for one country are rewritten and reenacted using actors and sets that reflect local life elsewhere in the world. These, in turn, often form the basis for locally produced spin-offs. Crucially for Robertson, glocalization gives rise to new products that feed back into global culture. This happens when a local adaption of a major commodity is exported to other cultures and adapted further still.

⬆ **World market**
Glocalization puts a local spin on well-known, branded products.

LOCAL PROBLEM UNTANGLED

One of the world's largest manufacturers of domestic appliances adjusted the technology of its washing machines to meet a local need. A new agitator designed for the Indian market altered the washing action, enabling women to launder their long saris without them becoming tangled up.

SASKIA SASSEN

1949–

Born in the Hague, in the Netherlands, Saskia Sassen is a Dutch-American sociologist and a professor of sociology at Columbia University. A leading figure in urban sociology, she is noted for her work on globalization, migration, and social inequality. Sassen is best known for her book *The Global City*, published in 1991, which examines the impact of globalization on the people who live and work in modern cities.

A GLOBAL TRAVELER

During World War II, Sassen's father worked as a member of a Nazi propaganda unit. In 1948, her family fled to Argentina with other high-ranking members of the Nazi party. As a child, Sassen's family moved frequently. She was raised in Argentina and Italy and later studied in France and the US. Her own experiences as a global traveler shaped her work on modern cities and the problems of urban life.

GLOBAL CITIES

Sassen's book, *The Global City*, looks at the way certain cities—notably New York, London, and Tokyo—have become centers of the global economy. Yet, in spite of their vast scale and size, these cities are made up of many distinct, smaller areas, each with its own cultural identity. Sassen's work focuses on the impact global cities have on local communities, where many of the inhabitants suffer from poverty, prejudice, and social injustice.

TAKING TO THE STREETS

Sassen uses the term "global street" to refer to public spaces where people from poor or disadvantaged communities, such as migrant and low-wage workers, can make their voices heard. She argues that protests in traditional places—such as town centers or public parks—have lost their impact and are no longer effective. Instead, Sassen calls for people to protest in the urban streets where they live and work.

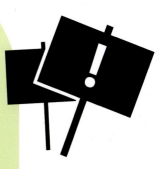

"The **street** is a **space** where new forms of the **social** and the **political** can be made."

GUESTS AND ALIENS

Much of Sassen's writing focuses on the problems of immigration. In her book *Guests and Aliens* (1999), Sassen explores the ways various migrant groups have been treated in different countries. Sassen calls for a fairer approach to immigration— one that benefits the host society as well as the migrant communities, many of whom have been forced to leave their homelands because of war or persecution.

A talented linguist, Sassen was raised speaking Spanish, Italian, French, Dutch, and German—she has also studied Russian and Japanese.

What's our **IMPACT** on the **PLANET**?

IT IS EASY TO BELIEVE THAT ENVIRONMENTAL PROBLEMS SUCH AS CLIMATE CHANGE ARE SOMETHING FOR THE SCIENTISTS TO SORT OUT. AFTER ALL, AREN'T THE BIG INDUSTRIES TO BLAME? BUT THE TRUTH IS THAT OUR "BUY IT AND TRASH IT" LIFESTYLES HAVE A MAJOR IMPACT ON THE HEALTH OF THE PLANET. DIRECTLY OR INDIRECTLY, ORDINARY PEOPLE ARE CONTRIBUTING TO GLOBAL CHANGES.

Managing waste

Waste disposal doesn't end when the barrels are emptied. It involves transport and, for non-recyclable materials, methods such as incineration or landfilling that contribute to environmental pollution.

WE DON'T HAVE A SOCIETY IF WE DESTROY THE ENVIRONMENT.

MARGARET MEAD, US ANTHROPOLOGIST

Warming world

Since the 1960s, environmentalists and other scientists have been warning us that human activities are directly contributing to the warming of Earth's climate. They claim that rising levels of greenhouse gas emissions, brought about by industrial processes such as burning fossil fuels and the emission of carbon dioxide from car exhaust fumes, are the main cause for the general rise in temperatures all over the world. As modern industries grow and spread, their impact on the global environment massively intensifies year by year.

Throwaway societies

Environmental sociologists analyze how social structures such as the legal system, the economy, and political policy impact on the environment. British expert Anthony Giddens believes that many people hold the idea that climate change is something happening at world level and therefore outside their control. He emphasizes that, on the contrary, environmental problems are inextricably bound up with our everyday lifestyles.

In his book *The Politics of Climate Change*, written in 2009, Giddens focuses on the effects of consumerism on the environment. In capitalist societies our lives are likely to be organized around the consumption of material goods and services, of which waste is an inherent part. Much of what we buy, such as food, clothes, and household goods, comes in packaging that is thrown away once the items are "consumed." An average household might dump the equivalent of six trees' worth of paper a year in the form of newspapers, packaging, and junk mail. The fact that natural resources will not last forever fundamentally undermines the sustainability of a capitalist society based around consumption of mass-produced goods.

Working for change

Another British sociologist of the environment, Philip Sutton, finds that increasing numbers of people are taking a critical look at their own consumer habits and doing something to change them. One response is to use organic and locally sourced foodstuffs. This eliminates large-scale production, reducing greenhouse gas emissions produced by the transport of goods. Local councils and communities are also taking more responsibility for the environment, putting their collective energies into initiatives that include ride sharing, communal gardening areas, community clean-up days, and recycling drives.

Every year, 8.8 million tons of plastic waste ends up in the world's oceans.

Environmental racism

Factors such as class and ethnic origins mean that some social groups are more likely than others to suffer from environmental changes. People in poorer parts of the world like southeast Asia and India are the worst hit by consequences such as rising sea levels, drought, or flooding. Developing countries can also be affected by the demands of first-world consumerist societies. The felling of rainforests for timber or to clear land for megacrops destroys the lifestyles of local peoples. Significant areas of Brazilian rainforest are cut down to provide grazing for cattle, whose meat is then shipped to Europe. Sociologists call this uneven distribution of the effects of environmental change "environmental racism."

So what we do on one side of the world may have an impact on the other side. Only global cooperation can effectively slow down environmental change. While the industrial sector has a heavy responsibility, the part played by ordinary people matters, too.

See also: 116–117, 118–119

IF WE THROW AWAY THE WORLD, WE CAN'T BUY A NEW ONE.

LOW-IMPACT LIVING

Eco-homes could ease the pressure on the planet. Built from reclaimed, non-polluting materials and using renewable solar energy, they have a low environmental impact. But British-based scholar Jenny Pickerill believes such homes will not become a model for the future until we learn to actively seek lifestyle changes, and not expect amenities such as instant hot water at all times.

ANTHONY GIDDENS

1938–

Regarded as one of Britain's leading sociologists, Anthony Giddens has written more than 35 books on a wide range of subjects, including psychology, economics, linguistics, anthropology, and politics. He is best known for his theory of structuration, which explores the relationship between individuals and social structures—such as religion and social class. He is also noted for his ideas on human identity, globalization, and climate change.

A MAN OF MANY WORDS

Giddens was born and raised in north London. He studied sociology and psychology at Hull University, then went on to the London School of Economics and Cambridge University, where he later became a professor of sociology. As well as writing hundreds of books and articles, he also cofounded the academic publishing house Polity Press. During the 1990s, he became an adviser to British Prime Minister Tony Blair.

> A passionate soccer supporter, Giddens wrote his thesis at the London School of Economics on "Sport and Society in Contemporary England."

SELF-IDENTITY

In his 1990 book *The Consequences of Modernity*, Giddens examines how people gain a sense of their own identity. In traditional societies, self-identity was largely shaped by a person's religion or social class. As these types of social systems have become less influential, people have had to make sense of their own identity. Giddens claims that self-identity has become a "reflexive" process, meaning that people have to reflect constantly on who they are and what defines them.

THE **THIRD WAY**

In recent years, Giddens has played a major role in global politics. In his book *The Third Way* (1998), Giddens outlined his ideas for a new model of politics that aimed to create a fairer society. Instead of relying on the traditional divisions of left-wing and right-wing politics, he argued for a "Third Way"—a political system that encouraged growth and wealth creation, while ensuring greater social justice and equal opportunities.

> **"** People find it hard to give the **same level of reality** to the **future** as they do to the **present**.**"**

GLOBAL WARMING

In *The Politics of Climate Change* (2009), Giddens warns of the risks of ignoring climate change. He argues that because the effects of global warming are not immediately visible in everyday life, people are reluctant to take action. Yet, if we wait for environmental catastrophes—such as massive floods, rising sea levels, and higher temperatures—to occur, it will be too late to do anything about them. This dilemma is known as the "Giddens' Paradox."

COLONIAL LEGACY

Many of the world's inequalities can be traced back to the colonial legacy of European nations such as Britain, France, Spain, Portugal, and the Netherlands. In the 17th and 18th centuries, traders sailed to Africa, South America, and the Caribbean for exotic goods and slaves to sell. Setting up colonies also allowed Europeans to exploit the resources of these countries.

GLOBAL GOODS

The world's first McDonald's outside of the US opened in British Columbia, Canada, in 1967. McDonald's outlets can now be found in 119 countries across the globe. The global reach of Coca Cola extends farther. It can be bought everywhere except North Korea and Cuba, although it has been smuggled into Cuba.

Wealth and development
IN CONTEXT

LOW-COST AIR TRAVEL

The rise in the number of people traveling abroad was made possible by the emergence of low-cost airlines during the late 1980s. Air travel became possible for people who in the past would not have been able to afford to fly, although the environmental consequences of increased air traffic have been significant.

SLOW FOOD MOVEMENT

First founded in Piedmont, Italy, in 1986, the Slow Food Movement is a worldwide organization aimed at ensuring that local food cultures do not disappear in the wake of globalization. The aims of the organization are to try to ensure that eating traditions and national cuisines continue to flourish.

CELEBRITY CULTURE

In his book, *Celebrity* (2001), British sociologist Chris Rojek discusses the influence of celebrity culture. Rojek's work analyzes the ambiguous status of modern celebrities. While they serve as role models for many, at the same time they bring into sharp focus the vast disparities in wealth and social power at the heart of modern culture.

ACID RAIN

In *World Risk Society* (1999), German sociologist Ulrich Beck's analysis shows the risks of environmental damage. Pollution from the industrially advanced countries of Western Europe and North America has effects around the globe. For example, rain made acidic by atmospheric pollution in one country damages lakes and marshes thousands of miles away.

Sociologists seek to understand how and why inequalities exist in society. In the 19th and early 20th centuries, sociologists conducted many studies to understand inequalities between the social classes. More recently, they have analyzed differences in the economic and political power of nations and the impact of globalization.

FAIR TRADE

Established in 1992 in London, the Fair Trade Foundation encourages consumers to buy goods and services at a price that is fair for the overseas growers. Producers of crops such as coffee or cocoa receive a fair price for their product so as to help reduce poverty, encourage sustainability, and treat the farmers ethically.

IMPACT OF TOURISM

For countries such as Kenya, tourism provides a vital source of income. A study of Amboseli National Park, Kenya in the 1990s showed that a herd of elephants generated $610,000 (£487,000) in tourist revenue per year. However, the increasing numbers of tourists has a damaging effect on ecosystems, infrastructure, and cultural traditions.

Modern
CULTURE

I SHOP therefore I AM?

What is CULTURE?

LEISURE time

We are living in UNCERTAIN times

Does the MASS MEDIA affect YOU?

Who OWNS the MEDIA?

Who DECIDES what's NEWS?

WHERE do you get your NEWS from?

What does the INTERNET do for US?

Do you LIVE ONLINE?

Modern culture is made up of the ideas, habits, and activities that surround us. Our modern world moves fast, bringing ideas and news from around the globe. Sometimes information arrives so quickly and from so many different sources that it can be hard to take in. What makes news and who controls it are big questions for sociologists to ponder, as are the effects of the internet and social media.

See also: 14–15, 22–23

I **SHOP** therefore

IN MODERN SOCIETY, OUR PERSONAL IDENTITIES—THE WAY WE SEE OURSELVES AND OTHERS SEE US—ARE TO A LARGE EXTENT CREATED BY THE GOODS WE BUY AND USE. PEOPLE WHO LIVED IN EARLIER CENTURIES, WHEN CONSUMER OPTIONS WERE LIMITED, DREW THEIR SENSE OF SELF FROM THE HOMES, COMMUNITIES, AND REGIONS IN WHICH THEY LIVED.

Building an identity

Trying to understand who we are and how we would like to be seen by others takes up a lot of our time and energy. Our identity matters to us. This might seem like just part of being human, but preoccupation with self-image is a modern phenomenon directly connected to the rise of consumerism from the 20th century onward. In today's consumer society, people play an increasingly active role in constructing their self-identity.

In the past, your identity would have been decided by the family you were born into and your place in the community. It was not something within your control. A person's occupation was usually handed down from generation to generation. The children of farmers, for example, tended to become farmers, and the sons of doctors were likely to enter the medical profession. The region people came from gave them a strong sense of who they were, too. Religion was another powerful influence in shaping people's self-image and behavior, providing them with a shared stock of moral values, ideals, and attitudes. In the traditional societies of centuries past, personal identity was largely fixed.

By contrast, in modern society identity and selfhood are things we have to create for ourselves, which we do primarily through our choice of the goods and services we buy.

Statistics show that young people vote for shopping as their favorite pastime.

A style statement

We are bombarded with information and advertisements encouraging us to buy and use—consume—certain products, services, and lifestyles. For British sociologist Richard Jenkins, the role of the advertising industry is to create and attach symbolic value to products and services. The implication is that acquiring these things will confer on us socially desirable traits such as "sophistication," "style," and

FINDING OURSELVES

In his book *The Shopping Experience* (1997), British sociologist Colin Campbell explains that shopping, far from being frivolous, is as much about acquiring an understanding of ourselves as it is about acquiring goods. The sorting through, selecting, and making final decisions to buy certain items helps us to arrive at a clearer sense of our self-identity.

I am?

Expressing ourselves ⬇
Everything we buy, from "designer" jeans to branded cappuccinos, says something about our inner person.

WHAT DOES A LABEL REALLY SAY?

CONSUMPTION IS A SYMBOLIC SYSTEM.
DANIEL MILLER, BRITISH SOCIAL ANTHROPOLOGIST

"wealth." For example, the decision to buy one brand of shoes rather than another is not merely one of personal preference but meant to be read as an expression of our inner selves. Shoes can say we are discerning, cool, or geeky, or don't care what anybody thinks.

Shopping for an identity
In the 21st century, an ever greater part of our lives involves shopping. According to British social anthropologist Daniel Miller, many people enjoy shopping in itself, regardless of what they buy. This is because shopping for, say, clothes or food, is an opportunity for shaping our identity. To some consumers, a recent and important part of this building-up of self image is the range of portable activity trackers used to monitor physical progress, such as the number of steps taken per day. And while we shop, we have an arena such as the mall in which to communicate our identity to others. Anti-consumerist campaigners point to the environmental damage done by high levels of consumption. But, as Miller and others highlight, consumerism enables people to create an identity in ways that were denied them in the past.

See also: 14–15, 96–97, 124–125, 132–133, 146

What is CULTURE?

HIP-HOP OR OPERA? BOOKS OR BALL GAMES? THE IDEAS, ACTIVITIES, ARTS, AND BEHAVIOR THAT PEOPLE LOOSELY REFER TO AS CULTURE ARE USUALLY SEEN AS A MATTER OF PERSONAL TASTE. WE BELIEVE THAT OUR CHOICES ARE FREELY MADE, AND SAY SOMETHING ABOUT WHO WE ARE, BUT OUR LIKES AND DISLIKES MAY BE THE RESULT OF SUBTLE SOCIAL INFLUENCES.

Worldwide, the seven Harry Potter books have sold 400,000 million copies in 68 languages.

ALL TELEVISION SHOWS ARE GARBAGE.

ROCK SINGERS DON' UNDERSTAND GOO MUSIC.

See also: 14–15, 34–35, 56–57

The "habitus"

The way culture shapes people's minds and bodies was central to the work of French sociologist Pierre Bourdieu. He coined the term "habitus" to refer to the lifestyle and cultural tastes characteristic of a specific social class. He argued that people born into a particular group become socialized into its habitus. In part, this is consciously directed by group members. For example, parents and friends are likely to promote and share their preferences for, say, sports or music. But, for the most part, being absorbed into the habitus takes place at a subconscious level. This is a key idea for Bourdieu—that the habitus shapes how we think and act in ways we rarely stop to think about. The relationship of an individual to the habitus is one Bourdieu described as "second nature." It just seems natural and self-evident that we like certain styles and activities and dislike others.

Choices

When people say they prefer one thing to another (perhaps listening to soul rather than folk rock, or eating an avocado rather than a pizza), they think that their cultural tastes are an expression of who they are. According to Bourdieu, nothing could be further from the truth. He acknowledged that we do actively make choices all the time about the lifestyles and consumer goods we like and dislike. What we do not choose, he said, are the social influences and cultural patterns that shape our values. It is the habitus of the group to which we belong that determines our choices, rather than our own individually acquired tastes.

CULTURAL OMNIVORES

In 1992, US sociologist Richard Peterson introduced the idea of the "cultural omnivore." He showed how tastes change when differences between class-based cultures blur. Cultural interests once assumed of the upper class, like art and theater, and the lower class, like sports, are now likely to be enjoyed more equally by people from all types of social groups.

Group input

As we grow up, we unconsciously absorb many cultural ideas from the social group in which we live. This early input is influential in shaping our future tastes and preferences.

BOOKS ARE BORING.

IT'S OK FOR MEN TO DO BALLET.

ORGANIC FOOD IS WORTH THE COST.

TRY EVERYTHING! YOU DON'T KNOW WHAT YOU MIGHT LIKE!

OPERA IS ONLY FOR RICH PEOPLE.

MODERN ART REALLY MAKES YOU STOP AND THINK.

WHERE DID THAT IDEA COME FROM?

Class and culture

To demonstrate his ideas, Bourdieu carried out a large-scale study in 1979, which he called "Distinction." The study examined the cultural tastes and preferences of a large cross section of French individuals. Drawing on a broad range of data taken from statistical methods, interviews, and participant observation, Bourdieu found that the cultural preferences and tastes of the individuals were strongly shaped by their class. On the whole, individuals with an upper-middle-class habitus tended to prefer certain cultural forms and pursuits, such as classical music, ballet, and fine art. At the same time, this group expressed a strong dislike for other types of culture such as rock concerts and soccer games. By contrast, individuals with a lower-class habitus tended to express a dislike for ballet and opera, preferring to socialize in bars and go to the movies.

THE POINT OF MY WORK IS TO SHOW THAT CULTURE AND EDUCATION AREN'T SIMPLY HOBBIES OR MINOR INFLUENCES.

PIERRE BOURDIEU, FRENCH SOCIOLOGIST

Predictable preferences

Bourdieu's work is intended to demonstrate the highly predictable nature of cultural preferences. The "Distinction" study suggests that our individual tastes are not an expression of self-identity, but of social class. Bourdieu does not say that some cultural pursuits are superior to or more sophisticated than others. Rather, he pointed out that what we understand as the most intimate expressions of self—our cultural likes and dislikes—are in fact influenced by a range of factors such as class, gender, and ethnic origin. For the most part, we remain unaware of these influences.

See also: 126–127, 128–129

PIERRE BOURDIEU

1930–2002

French sociologist Pierre Bourdieu began his academic career as a philosopher before becoming interested in sociology. During his career, he wrote more than 30 books and 300 articles on a wide range of subjects including art history, education, and literary criticism. His best-known book, *Distinction* (1979), explored the role of social class in modern society. A harsh critic of social inequality, Bourdieu was an active social and political campaigner.

CLIMBING THE LADDER

Bourdieu was born into a working-class family in rural France. His father was a postal worker who encouraged him to work hard at school. A brilliant student, he went on to study philosophy at the École Normale Supérieure in Paris. Throughout his career, Bourdieu was conscious that his modest upbringing was very different compared to the privileged backgrounds of his colleagues. It was this awareness that shaped his lifelong interest in social equality and justice.

A SENSE OF BELONGING

Bourdieu is most famous for his ideas on "habitus." He used this term to describe a "sense of belonging" to a certain social group or class. Bourdieu recognized that people of the same social class develop similar views on life from an early age. They learn to speak and act in a similar way as their family and friends, and tend to share the same kinds of interests and values.

CAPITAL GAINS

Bourdieu claimed that each person's habitus is made up of different amounts of "capital." Economic capital, for example, refers to money and wealth. Cultural capital includes speech, education, and manners or a person's taste in music or art. Social capital refers to a person's network of friends or colleagues. For Bourdieu, the amount of capital people have determines how successful they will be in life.

While teaching at the University of Algeria, Bourdieu conducted fieldwork on the people of the Kabylia region, which led to his first book, *The Sociology of Algeria* (1958).

"Cultural needs are the product of upbringing and education."

ENTERING THE FIELD

According to Bourdieu, social inequality exists because different social groups have different amounts of capital. He developed the idea that society is divided into "fields"—such as business, law, or education—each with its own set of rules. To enter a particular field, people need different types of capital. Bourdieu argued that people with capital such as wealth, academic qualifications, or social connections find it easier to enter certain fields.

LEISURE time

MOST PEOPLE AGREE THAT TIME OFF OF WORK IS A GOOD THING, AND THAT WE DON'T HAVE ENOUGH. YET WE HAVE MANY MORE FREE HOURS IN A DAY THAN EARLIER GENERATIONS COULD EVER HAVE IMAGINED, AND A VAST LEISURE INDUSTRY TO HELP US FILL THEM. THE LEISURE ACTIVITIES WE CHOOSE CAN MAKE A DIFFERENCE TO OUR HEALTH, OUR SENSE OF IDENTITY, AND EVEN OUR CAREERS.

More time off

Going away on vacation or simply taking days off of school or work is something we all look forward to. Leisure time is "me-time," away from the stresses and struggles of everyday life. The idea of leisure has changed dramatically in the last century. At one time, the term "leisure class" meant members of the upper class, or the very wealthy— people with plenty of money and not much to do. To many people of earlier generations, leisure first and foremost simply meant not having to work. It was time used to recover from the daily grind and concentrate on easier, family-centered activities. Leisure had little to do with cultivating wider interests or pursuing sports and adventures.

Since the turn of the 20th century, legal and political reforms have led to shorter working hours. With a greater understanding of the effects of overwork on health, we now recognize that everyone needs time off. We may never seem to have enough leisure, but we do have far more spare time than the workers of a century ago.

The leisure culture

An important part of increased leisure time is the growth of a consumer culture that makes a significant contribution to the national economy. According to sociologist Chris Rojek,

See also: 18–19, 22–23, 60–61, 96–97

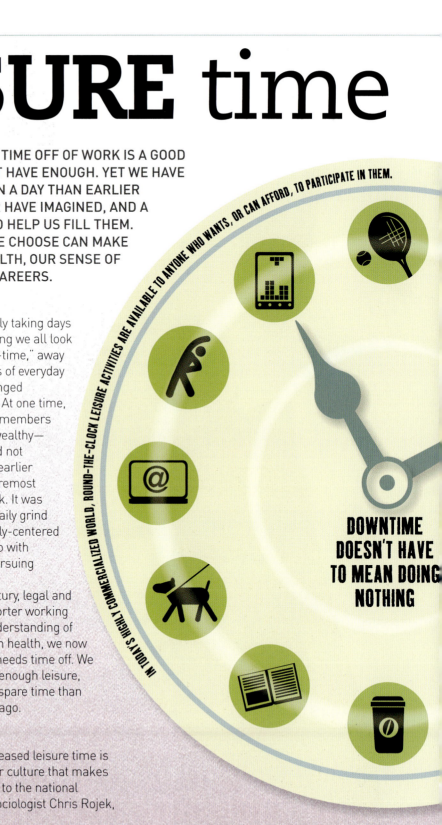

IN TODAY'S HIGHLY COMMERCIALIZED WORLD, ROUND-THE-CLOCK LEISURE ACTIVITIES ARE AVAILABLE TO ANYONE WHO WANTS, OR CAN AFFORD, TO PARTICIPATE IN THEM.

DOWNTIME DOESN'T HAVE TO MEAN DOING NOTHING

The US tourism industry generated $1.5 trillion in economic output in 2016.

modern society is unique in that it has given rise to a vast industry based around leisure activities. For many people—such as hotel staff, movie theater workers, and airline pilots—leisure is a source of employment. For others, time off work is an opportunity for spending money on goods and services. Exotic vacations (and shopping for the clothes and accessories to go with them), outings to theme parks, and trips to the theater are examples of pursuits around which the commercial leisure industry has grown, generating sums of money that would have been unimaginable to many living just a few decades ago.

Positive or negative effects?

People often put as much time and energy into saving for, planning, and engaging in leisure pursuits as they do into their jobs. However, similar to the inequalities in pay between the men and women, women tend to receive less leisure time than men. This may be because more men work full time and so accrue more time off. Today, leisure is less likely to mean inactivity, and more likely about doing and seeing things that stretch us physically and mentally. What we do in our time off is of increasing interest to our

THE BEST INTELLIGENCE TEST IS WHAT WE DO WITH OUR LEISURE.
LAURENCE J. PETER, CANADIAN AUTHOR

employers. For example, pursuits involving physical exercise or team sports are understood to positively impact our working lives, perhaps developing our capacity to work as part of a group as well as keeping us fit and healthy. Mention of such pursuits could add interest to a résumé. On the other hand, spending leisure time in excessive socializing, or doing nothing, might be viewed negatively as apathy or lack of initiative. How we spend our leisure time is increasingly regarded as an expression of our identity, no less than the jobs we do and the professional roles we occupy.

See also: 133, 144–145

NEW SPORT, NEW IDENTITY

New Zealand sociologist Holly Thorpe's research (2011) looked at how the increasing popularity of snowboarding drew many women to a once exclusively male sport. Thorpe's work suggested that women started to feel differently about themselves as they become an accepted part of the snowboarding scene. They acquired new confidence and a passion that fed into other areas of their lives, particularly work.

◉ Choosing an activity

What we choose to do with our leisure time can reflect our identity. Sometimes, a physically or mentally demanding activity can create a new and stronger identity.

⊘ Swept along
Being in the fast-moving "liquid" flow of modern life can feel like being caught up in a river, carried along by something that we cannot control.

LIFE IN OUR MODERN WORLD IS FAST-PACED, UNCERTAIN, AND CONSTANTLY CHANGING. IT HAS BEEN DESCRIBED AS A "LIQUID" TIME. WE MAY EXPERIENCE THIS FLOW AS EXHILARATING AND OCCASIONALLY OVERWHELMING. PRODUCTS AND PEOPLE TRAVEL AROUND THE GLOBE, TAKING BELIEFS AND VALUES WITH THEM, BRINGING DISPARATE THINGS TOGETHER, AND FORMING NEW SITUATIONS AND EXPERIENCES.

WE LIVE IN A FAST-FLOWING "LIQUID MODERNITY"

A liquid world

Polish sociologist Zygmunt Bauman described life in our fast-moving world as like living in "liquid" times. Bauman is trying to capture the fluidity and formlessness of human experience in the global capitalist society. In this liquid world, people, goods, and cultural beliefs flow across the world more freely than ever before, giving rise to new ideas and experiences. Supermarkets stock exotic food items from all over the world, all-year round. A routine knee operation in a US hospital may involve being cared for by a nurse from Poland and a surgeon from Dubai, using surgical instruments made in Germany. Our everyday lives depend on the flow of people and knowledge around the world. Many people we interact with and rely on are unknown to us and yet we have little option but to trust them. Bauman sees this as both terrifying and exhilarating.

In a survey, US citizens were found to be the least likely to choose to find work overseas.

On solid ground

For a generation of young people in the developed world, this is just how life is. But life was not always like this. As recently as thirty years ago, lifestyles were more fixed. Bauman describes the period from the end of World War II to the 1990s as "heavy modernity." During this time, social life was more predictable and ordered. Many people grew up and lived in the same geographical area where they were born. They often worked in the same job until they retired. Their identity was rooted in the jobs they did, the class they came from, and the communities and nation they belonged to. Relationships were more enduring, too. Marriage rates were higher, divorce rates lower, and friendships were rooted in the community.

Flowing and merging

By contrast, liquid modern life is uncertain, unpredictable, and fast-moving. Bauman identifies the rise of the internet, the economic and political power of

We are living in

transnational corporations (see pp108–9), and low-cost air travel as driving the transition from heavy to liquid modernity.

In a liquid modern world, all that was fixed and solid becomes changeable and fluid. Flows of people from all over the world cross national boundaries in search of new and better lives. Environmental

> ## IN A LIQUID LIFE THERE ARE NO PERMANENT BOUNDS.
>
> ### ZYGMUNT BAUMAN, POLISH SOCIOLOGIST

disasters and wars force people to relocate and rebuild their lives in locations far away from where they were born.

The flow of consumer goods and services allows us to put together our own identity, buying items from around the world and creating a look and character we desire, if we can afford it. Fashion and lifestyles from different cultures come into contact and merge with one another, giving rise to new hybrid fashions and cultural trends. Human relationships can be more readily formed but are more fleeting. People from all over the globe come into contact, either face-to-face, or virtually, as they

CHANGE AND ANXIETY

The speed of social and economic change in a global world has led to rising levels of fear and unease among the members of modern societies. Official statistics show that in 1980, 4% of people in the US suffered from a mental disorder connected with anxiety. As of 2016, almost half of Americans did. The statistics demonstrate the relationship between psychological states and fast-paced social change.

become part of online communities and networks, before moving on and making new connections with others.

Moving too fast

Although often exhilarating, Bauman sees the pace of liquid life, for most of us, as unsettling. Liquid life moves too fast for all but well-off members of a transnational elite. Like global tourists, these people are able to make the most of the opportunities that the liquid life offers. By contrast, the majority of people experience the speed of social, political, and economic change as overwhelming and anxiety-provoking.

See also: 108–109, 110–111, 132–133

UNCERTAIN times

ZYGMUNT BAUMAN

1925–2017

Born in Poland into a Jewish family, Zygmunt Bauman was regarded as one of the most influential sociologists of the 20th century. Expelled from Poland in 1968, he moved first to Israel, then settled in England in 1971, where he became a professor of sociology at Leeds University. He published more than 50 books on a wide range of issues including consumerism, globalization, and the uncertain nature of modern society.

PERSECUTION AND EXILE

Bauman was born into a poor family in Poznan, west Poland. When the Nazis invaded Poland in 1939, Bauman fled with his family to Russia, where he later fought against the Nazis with a Polish regiment. In 1968, he was exiled a second time, when the Polish Communist Party expelled thousands of Jewish intellectuals. He eventually found refuge in England, where he remained for the rest of his career.

Bauman was awarded the Polish Military Cross of Valor for his bravery during World War II. He later became one of the youngest majors in the Polish army.

THE HOLOCAUST

In his controversial work *Modernity and the Holocaust* (1989), Bauman examines how it was possible for the Holocaust to happen. He argued that the mass murder of Jewish people, and others, was not simply an extreme case of barbaric behavior, specific to Germany. In Bauman's view, it was the rational and organized nature of modern society that made the Holocaust possible.

LIQUID MODERNITY

In the 1990s, Bauman developed his theory of "liquid modernity," which describes how the "fluid" and changeable nature of modern society has left people feeling insecure (see pp128–9). According to Bauman, society has moved away from the "solid modernity" of the industrialized 19th century—a period that was relatively stable and predictable. In Bauman's view, we are now living in an age of constant uncertainty and increasing levels of risk.

"If you **define** your value by the things you **acquire** and surround yourself with, being excluded is **humiliating**."

WE ARE WHAT WE BUY

Bauman was interested in the way modern "liquid" society has affected personal identity. Up until the 1970s, people tended to define themselves by what they did for a living. In today's society, however, the idea of a "job for life" is no longer realistic. Bauman argued that personal identity in modern society is linked to consumerism—people now define themselves by the goods they buy and surround themselves with.

Does the **MASS MEDIA** affect **YOU**?

Getting involved
When we watch the news, we interpret the coverage according to a variety of factors, such as our age, ethnicity, and gender.

WE ARE NOT A PASSIVE AUDIENCE

"MASS MEDIA" REFERS TO THE BUSINESSES AND ORGANIZATIONS THAT PROVIDE US WITH NEWS AND INFORMATION. THEY HAVE AN INFLUENTIAL ROLE. BUT DOES IT REALLY MATTER WHAT THEY TELL US?

Is the media biased?

From politicians to the police, and parents to schoolteachers, concerns about how the media influences the minds of the public, particularly those of young people, is the cause of much debate. The media purports to be passing on to its audience facts rather than opinion. However, how objective is it? During the two world wars, we know that the Nazi Party used the media to control the flow of news to the German people, distorting the words of anyone who disagreed with it. Around the world during times of conflict there is similar concern that the media is not passing on the truth but has a point of view of its own, a bias.

Young adults spend up to 27 hours a week online. Adults spend up to 20 hours, including those spent using the internet at work.

See also: 136–137, 138–139, 140–141, 146–147

Speaking with one voice

It is hard to deny that the media affects us all at some level. In our digital world, news about events taking place across the globe reaches us, via our phone, laptop, TV screen, or newspaper, wherever we are. However, for sociologists of the media, the notion that "the media" comprises a single, all-powerful entity that talks to everyone in an undifferentiated way is one that requires careful analysis. In actuality, the media comprises multiple news agencies and broadcasting companies that compete with one another for audience ratings. In order to maximize their ratings, media organizations publish a variety of news stories in different styles and formats, varying the political angle they adopt, and the style of reporting, to reach a range of audiences.

A passive audience?

In trying to understand the effects of the media, sociologists question the notion that audience members are "passive." This view supposes that the minds of the public uncritically absorb news and information, which shapes how they think and act in ways they are unaware of. Sociologists draw attention instead to the active role audience members play in interpreting the news. Instead of one big group, sociologists describe the recipients of media news as various "audiences." These audiences are differentiated by ethnicity, social class, age, and gender. Different news stories lead to various interpretations or "readings" by members of these different audiences.

In an analysis of the US mass media by sociologist Herbert Gans entitled *Deciding What's News* (1979), he found that some powerful media figures assumed that the US public comprised two types of viewer: an educated and affluent elite and a poorly educated and passive majority. Through interviews and time spent observing a cross section of the US public, Gans found that irrespective of their social background, news audiences adopt a critical stance toward the news they receive. Rather than the media coverage determining the views of the audience, audience members are actively involved in constructing meaning. Gans found that interpretations of the coverage of political events varied along gender and ethnic lines, with black Americans often adopting a critical stance toward the framing of

IRRITATION MEANS GETTING THE AUDIENCE INVOLVED, NOT JUST PASSIVE.

REUVEN FRANK, NBC NEWS DEVELOPER

news stories by predominantly white news editors and producers. The age of viewers also shaped an interpretation of the news, with older viewers demonstrating a concern for issues they perceived to have wider social and political consequences.

Gans' work provides strong evidence to contradict the view that the media can influence the minds of all of its audience.

SOAP OPERAS

A study by US sociologist Alan Rubin of the viewers of US soap operas found that the mainly female viewers watch not only to pass the time, but also because the moral issues the soap operas raise provide the basis for discussions with friends and colleagues. By looking at the soap operas with a critical eye, viewers reflect on their own moral perspectives.

Who owns the **MEDIA**?

EVERY MORNING MANY OF US WAKE TO HEAR THE NEWS ON THE RADIO OR TELEVISION, OR WE READ IT IN NEWSPAPERS OR ON OUR PHONES. MEDIA COMPANIES PLAY A MAJOR ROLE IN COMMUNICATING NEWS AND INFORMATION TO US. BUT DOES IT MATTER WHO OWNS THESE BUSINESSES? DOES IT AFFECT THE NEWS WE RECEIVE?

> The Murdoch family owns newspapers in Australia, the UK, and the US, plus many TV channels.

The media matters

Knowledge of what is happening across the world and how this will impact our lives is vital in our global society. It matters because we may have friends or family who live in other countries, we may work for a company with colleagues in offices overseas, we may wonder how world events will affect the global financial markets, or we may be making travel plans. But how reliable is the news and information we receive from the media? Do the people who own and run the media have an effect on the news that we receive?

US sociologist Noam Chomsky would say that the powerful individuals and corporations who own the media use it to influence the population. Using a range of statistical data and public information, Chomsky demonstrates that ownership of the media in the US is concentrated in the hands of a very rich and powerful minority. Of the approximately 25,000 corporate and independent news producers in the US, the richest 29, which include several major media corporations, account for over half the output of news.

Making a profit

Chomsky claims that media outlets reinforce the beliefs and values that are shared by businesses, institutions, and the media, and avoids being critical of these relationships and culture. Media organizations are businesses that

Media domination

There are a few powerful media companies who own a wealth of media outlets around the world.

are owned by their shareholders who demand that they make a profit, and any that are not financially sustainable will go out of business. Chomsky draws attention to what he calls the "filters" that shape how media content is chosen and presented in order to keep the company solvent.

The primary filter is advertising. Money derived from advertising strongly influences how and what the media reports. News stories with negative messages about businesses that are paying large sums of money to advertise with the news company present a dilemma. Criticism of the company would threaten the likelihood of future advertising deals.

See also: 48–49, 134–135, 138–139, 140–141

that make people question the credibility of these people or institutions. Businesses or governments may feel threatened by this. Chomsky believes powerful media organizations are actively involved in spreading fear by identifying and demonizing anyone who is critical of their powerful status.

The second filter is sourcing. Political news often comes from press releases issued by government officials. Media firms that provide negative coverage of the government's policies are likely to be excluded from these meetings in the future. A third filter is fear. Investigative journalists may uncover stories about individuals and institutions

Citizen journalists

The widespread use of new media has begun to challenge the power of the media organizations. Portable devices such as mobile phones and tablets mean that events can be easily recorded, and this coverage can be readily distributed through file-sharing websites. While footage on a handheld device is not of the same quality or as verifiable as professional news reports, alternative accounts of events provided by citizen journalists or members of the public challenge the view that powerful media monopolies are the only source of valid information in the modern world.

THE MEDIA ARE A CORPORATE MONOPOLY...

NOAM CHOMSKY, US SOCIOLOGIST

Who DECIDES

IN THE COURSE OF A DAY, MOST PEOPLE ACCESS AT LEAST ONE SOURCE OF NEWS INFORMATION. HOWEVER YOU FIND THE NEWS, VIA A NEWSPAPER, THE TELEVISION, OR A MOBILE APP, WHAT COUNTS AS NEWS AND HOW THE CONTENTS OF THE NEWS ARE SHAPED BY SOCIAL FACTORS ARE LONG-STANDING CONCERNS FOR SOCIOLOGISTS.

NEWS MACHINE

1. Events take place
"News" events are happening all the time but our news reports only include those that are selected by journalists, editors, and media owners.

2. Telling the story
The event is shaped by journalists whose accounts will be influenced by social and cultural factors, such as the age, class, gender, religion, or ethnicity of the journalist and the audience.

3. Outside factors
"Structural" elements, such as the size of the news company or the cost of covering a story, will also affect the choice of stories transmitted.

News selection

The stories covered by television news bulletins, posted on news websites, and featured in the pages of newspapers, are the products of a selection process. Which stories to include, which headlines to use, and whether certain information is dropped or kept in, is all decided by a range of interpersonal, organizational, and wider social processes. How these combine to shape the structure and content of the news is important to sociologists who study the media. US sociologist Richard Petersen claimed that the news is neither impartial nor objective. Rather, the contents of news stories is socially constructed.

More than 2.5 billion people read a printed newspaper regularly.

Petersen is not claiming that the news is less "real" or "true" as a result. Any account of a situation or event is affected by social factors such as the class, ethnicity, age, and gender of the person telling the story. These factors shape how all people interpret the world around them, and that includes journalists.

Gatekeepers of the news

Drawing on Petersen's ideas, US sociologist of the media Michael Schudson adds that the stories and information presented by the media are always the outcome of a range of "selective processes." These are the decisions made by media "gatekeepers": the journalists, camera operators, editors, and owners of news media outlets.

what's news?

All these gatekeepers, either alone or as part of an organization, play a part in determining what ends up in the news. The decisions they make include which news events to attend on a particular day, how to cover them, and which to drop in the final editing process.

Other pressures

There are also impersonal, structural factors that shape the contents of the news. These can have an effect even though the people who produce the news are unaware of them. They include the economic and organizational constraints that the gatekeepers of news operate within.

Particularly significant are financial constraints. The cost of sending news teams to foreign destinations strongly influences the decision of news corporations, particularly smaller independent organizations, to include a story or not. The amount of "air time" or newspaper column space available to editors is also a factor.

Research by sociologists based at the University of Glasgow (UK), known as the Glasgow Media Group, found that television news editors prefer to include soundbites of speech or live footage from the scene of the story, and stories that include these are more likely to be broadcast. This indicates that media

> **NEWS IS WHAT SOMEBODY SOMEWHERE WANTS TO SUPPRESS; ALL THE REST IS ADVERTISING.**
> LORD NORTHCLIFFE, EARLY 20TH CENTURY, BRITISH PUBLISHER

producers are aware of their audience, who feel that including information directly from the people involved in the story leads to a more authentic account.

The organizational structure of media companies directly shapes the contents of the news too. In independent media companies, the smaller staff means that there are fewer people involved in producing a story. This means that the final story is a more accurate portrayal of an individual journalist's approach to a particular story. This can be viewed either positively or negatively, but the story now reflects, in a more obvious way, the biases of the journalist.

See also: 134–135, 136–137, 140–141, 142–143

4. News report
The final story is the product of several processes, all of which have shaped what we read or see in the news.

NEWS IS FRESHLY MADE

A study called *The Media Elite* by researchers Lichter, Lichter, and Rothman (1986), supports Petersen's view that reality is socially constructed. News is not a factual report on the world; there is no "ready-made" reality waiting to be reported. The news is built from reports and opinions. The study suggests that the news should be imagined as a product that has to be freshly made each day.

Where do you get your **NEWS** from?

WHAT'S HAPPENING IN YOUR LOCAL AREA, AS WELL AS WHAT'S HAPPENING AROUND THE WORLD, IS AVAILABLE ON YOUR SMARTPHONE OR TABLET ALMOST AS SOON AS IT OCCURS. WHILE TELEVISION NEWS OR NEWSPAPERS ARE SLOWER, THEY MAY BE MORE RELIABLE.

What is "news"?

What is regarded as "news" likely varies depending on who you are. For young people, news might be whatever is trending on social media that day. For business owners, news might be the state of the stock market and the value of the dollar against the euro.

For most people, prior to the turn of the 19th century, news was usually information about local events. News often took the form of gossip, passed by word of mouth from one community member to another, or announced in the village square by the town crier. With the invention of newspapers in the late 17th century, national news was available, but only for a wealthy minority who were literate.

By the 1950s and 1960s, news was mainly conveyed through the radio and later television, both luxury items. By the 1970s, these were the main sources of news about the outside world for North American and Western European households.

There are an estimated 1.7 billion Facebook users around the world.

Is more news good news?

As news at a local, national, and international level became more accessible to all social groups, the amount of information presented to audiences grew too. Following the explosion of digital communications and the rise of the internet in the late 20th century, the amount of information available has meant that individuals can now seek out and find news that is relevant to them. This might mean following the movements of the stock market, getting updates from a favorite sports team, or reading the latest celebrity gossip. For Spanish sociologist Manuel Castells, the world's most economically and technologically advanced nations have entered the "Information Age." This means that there is now more activity around the production and consumption of information than for the mass-production of consumer goods.

See also: 136–137, 138–139

NEWS IS AVAILABLE FASTER

Is faster better?

The rise of internet-based technologies means that news is produced, distributed, and consumed faster than ever before. However, the reliability of this news is questionable. Not all organizations or individuals disseminating information spend time confirming the details or putting the facts into a wider context.

Many people are confronted with overwhelming amounts of information not just on a daily basis, but via minute-by-minute updates transmitted to audiences around the globe. More than ever before, people are involved in organizing and managing the amount and type of news they receive. The internet

MEDIA ATTACHMENT

British sociologist Michael Bull has studied the increasing importance people attach to new forms of media such as MP3 players and mobile phones. In his study, *Sound Moves: iPod Culture and the Urban Experience* (2007), he analyzes how new media devices have become so embedded in people's everyday experience that leaving home without them can be emotionally and psychologically stressful.

> # THE ADVANCEMENT AND DIFFUSION OF KNOWLEDGE IS THE ONLY GUARDIAN OF TRUE LIBERTY.
>
> JAMES MADISON, US PRESIDENT 1809–1817

means that regardless of where we are in the world or what time of day it is, news can be accessed by anyone with an internet connection from broadcasters located anywhere on the planet. As "new media," such as smartphones, computers, and other portable devices have become more affordable, compact, and embedded in everyday life, they have begun to replace television and newspapers. For younger people, advances in technology form part of the world they were born into. But the ease of use and affordability of new media means that they are an integral feature of the lives of people of all ages.

For US sociologist Matthew Hindman, technological advances have made news more "democratic," meaning that now people of all ages and from various social backgrounds can access it. Others fear that new media poses a threat: Information on the internet is often unregulated, so while it is more accessible than ever before, its reliability is difficult to discern.

See also: 142–143, 144–145

D MORE EASILY THAN EVER BEFORE

NEW MEDIA SOURCES SUCH AS SMARTPHONES AND TABLETS GIVE MORE PEOPLE ACCESS TO NEWS, BUT THE SPEED AND VOLUME OF INFORMATION AVAILABLE CAN BE OVERWHELMING.

What does the INTERNET DO for us?

THE INTERNET HAS CHANGED THE WORLD. WE CAN CONNECT WITH ALMOST ANYONE, ANYWHERE, ANY TIME. WE CAN ALSO USE THE NET AS A VAST SOURCE OF INFORMATION. BUT IS INTERNET TECHNOLOGY REALLY BRINGING US TOGETHER OR IS IT DRIVING SOME PEOPLE INTO ISOLATION? AND CAN WE TRUST WHAT WE READ ONLINE?

China was the first country to recognize internet addiction as a disorder, and to open special treatment facilities.

Network societies

We have entered the Information Age. That is what Spanish sociologist Manuel Castells says in his study *The Rise of the Network Society*, published in 1996. The central force behind this new era in our history is the internet. Up until the 1970s and 1980s, the economies of most developed societies were based on industrial-scale production of consumer goods and services. Since then, digital information, not goods, has become the main focus of what Castells calls "network societies." Internet-based technologies are driving social and cultural change.

A key idea for Castells is that the internet increases connectivity between people and places across the globe. Irrespective of anyone's social and ethnic background, the internet provides a virtual space in which people can link up with whomever they like, whenever and wherever they want. Provided you can get online, you can cross social barriers, timelines, and national boundaries via digital media.

THE INTERNET...ALLOWS THE COMMUNICATION OF MANY TO MANY...ON A GLOBAL SCALE.

MANUEL CASTELLS, SPANISH SOCIOLOGIST

LINKING UP

GETTING INFORMATION ON THE GO

TRAVELING AROUND

New identities and freedoms

For digital sociologist Deborah Lupton, the internet contributes to social solidarity and collective identity. She focuses in particular on the rise of virtual communities: online gamers who regularly link up to play computer games; political interest and activist groups; self-help forums; and chat-based sites through which people form relationships.

Lupton found that because the internet is anonymous, people feel free to express themselves in ways that they would find impossible in real life. This is particularly true for those who are pushed to the margins of society because of their identity, as may be the case with LGBT (lesbian, gay, bisexual, and transgender) groups and ethnic minorities.

Internet anxieties

Along with new freedoms, the internet has brought new concerns. Sources of information on websites are often unclear, so it can be difficult to tell whether online encyclopedias, for example, can be trusted. Anyone can post information or stories to serve personal interests.

Another common fear is that the internet isolates people by taking them out of the real world. US sociologist Paul DiMaggio investigated this concern in his 2001 study *Social Implications of the Internet*. He found that people who use the internet are more likely to call or visit friends than less frequent users. This is because heavy internet users do feel isolated, and so crave real human company. DiMaggio's work also shows that people who use the internet a lot are more likely to seek printed information from books and magazines. These findings are important in providing a perhaps unexpected account of how the internet shapes people's perceptions and behavior.

STAYING IN TOUCH

SHARING THE BIG MOMENT

These could include allegations against people, whether false or true, or damaging reviews of restaurants and other services.

An increasing anxiety for parents, according to sociologist Roy Charkalis, is the amount of time their children spend online. Social media is a very recent technological innovation, and rules and norms as to what usage is considered "normal" and acceptable have yet to be properly established.

⊕ **Connected**
Anywhere, anytime, the internet can be part of our social and cultural lives.

MEETING LIKE-MINDED PEOPLE

Do you live ONLINE?

SOCIAL MEDIA IS VERY IMPORTANT TO MANY YOUNG PEOPLE, WHO OFTEN COMMUNICATE MORE CONFIDENTLY THROUGH AN ONLINE IDENTITY THAN FACE TO FACE. INTERACTION VIA THE NET CAN BE SEEN AS A STEP TOWARD DEVELOPING RELATIONSHIPS IN REAL LIFE. BUT THERE ARE RISKS IN BEING PART OF A WORLDWIDE VIRTUAL SOCIETY.

More than 600,000 Facebook accounts are hacked into every day.

Creating an identity

An online, or virtual, identity is a collection of personal details about who and what you are. This may or may not be a true reflection of your "real life" self. Many young people create an online identity that they use to communicate with friends and family via popular social media sites such as Facebook, Instagram, Twitter, and Snapchat. US sociologist Sally McMillan says that learning to find your way around a network of online relationships can be seen as preparation for interacting with people in real society.

Online status matters

Going online blurs the boundaries between the personal and public dimensions of people's lives. What young people post on the internet can be a deliberately constructed version of themselves

THE INTERNET COULD BE A VERY POSITIVE STEP TOWARD EDUCATION AND PARTICIPATION IN A MEANINGFUL SOCIETY.

NOAM CHOMSKY, US SOCIOLOGIST

designed to raise their social prestige among their contemporaries. Pictures taken at a rock concert or on vacation, or selfies posing with a celebrity, are meant to impress, and tweaking reality for better effect is regarded as legitimate. Being seen positively online is vital for someone wanting to fit into peer groups and social networks. Winning approval from hundreds or even thousands of "followers" is a great boost to fragile self-esteem.

The pressure on people to maintain a constant online presence is growing. Experiencing what sociologists refer to as "digital exclusion" can spell social disaster. For example, being deprived of internet access or purposely excluded from chat groups may have a huge negative impact on young people.

The risks of a virtual world

The almost limitless scope for online social networking comes with certain risks. British sociologist Sonia Livingstone thinks this is particularly true in the case of young people and children, because the internet undermines their parents' capacity to regulate what they see and learn. Many publicly accessible sites do not have parental controls, and a child browsing online can inadvertently tap into inappropriate material.

Another risk is not being able to know the true identity of a person behind an online profile. Internet chat rooms and computer gaming communities can be and are infiltrated by predatory people looking to start up

SPYWARE FOR PARENTS

Parents are increasingly making use of devices that allow them to monitor what their children are doing online. A number of mobile phone apps have been developed that let parents follow a child's social media activities, legally "hack into" messages and photographs posted online, or even track a child's movements in the real world. Concerns have been raised that such so-called spyware could be exploited by the wrong people.

See also: 56–57, 142–143

"friendships" with the socially vulnerable, particularly young girls. What starts as a virtual relationship could become dangerously real.

Young people are also the most common victims of online crimes such as "trolling" and cyberbullying. These involve harassment and bullying of someone online by posting defamatory remarks, insults, and even threats. Anyone who puts personal details on, say, a blog or Facebook is an easy target.

For many young people, the internet is an indispensable tool for learning about social relationships. But in the virtual world, as in the real one, not everyone they meet will be quite what they seem.

CAUTION! DO YOU KNOW WHO YOU'RE REALLY TALKING TO?

◉ **Going public**
Creating a virtual identity blurs the distinction between private and public life. Remember: details on the internet can be anyone's business.

CULTURE INDUSTRY

Early sociologists of the media, such as the Frankfurt School (a group of sociologists in Germany in the 1930s), regarded the modern media as a cornerstone in the "Culture Industry." By this they were referring to the power of the organizations that decided on the news and stories that made up modern culture in the early 20th century.

CONSUMER SOCIETY

In the 1960s, the term "consumer society" began to enter mainstream culture. Material goods could now be manufactured on a vast scale, and were cheaper than ever before, enabling many more people to buy them. The advertising industry arose to generate desire for this new range of consumer goods and services.

Culture and the media
IN CONTEXT

THE MEDIUM IS THE MESSAGE

Canadian sociologist Marshall McLuhan developed the influential idea that "the medium is the message" in 1964. McLuhan was urging sociologists to focus attention on the medium of communication, not the content. In particular, he discussed television, which requires little input from the viewer but offers multiple sensory stimulation.

FIRST INTERNET

The first network of computers able to communicate with each other was created in 1969. This was ARPANET, or the Advanced Research Projects Agency Network. ARPANET involved four US universities working together to research how computer scientists could develop the technology necessary for worldwide, online connectivity. This was the start of the internet.

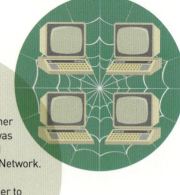

In 2016, the term "fake news" entered popular culture. Fake news includes information and reports that look like news, but are actually fabricated or misrepresented in an attempt to influence the opinions and attitudes of the public. Users of the internet can easily remain anonymous, making it easy to create and spread various kinds of disinformation.

FAKE NEWS

DECLINE OF NEWSPAPERS

The rise of the internet has had a negative impact on newspapers. In the last decade, newspaper publishers have struggled to compete with the immediacy and user-friendly format of online news websites and apps. The number of newspaper publishers that have closed, declared bankruptcy, or suffered severe cutbacks is rising, particularly in the US.

As society changes over time, culture also changes. When technological innovations catch on, they bring about changes in social relationships and cultural activities, too. Two of the main technological and cultural developments that have shaped modern society are the television and the internet.

SOCIAL NETWORKING

Social networking is an integral part of modern culture in the West. It is also popular in China, although the government has sought to control access to this technology. Launched in 2009, China's most popular social media platform, Weibo, is closely monitored, so it is primarily used for sharing jokes rather than posting news that could be controversial.

SOCIAL MEDIA

The rising popularity of internet-based social media is one of the defining features of modern culture. In 2004, Mark Zuckerberg and friends at Harvard University launched Facebook from a computer in their dorm on campus. Today, it is estimated that Facebook has 1.86 billion users worldwide.

Directory of sociologists

Jeffrey Alexander (1947–)

US sociologist Jeffrey Alexander is based at Yale University, where he is Codirector of the Center for Cultural Sociology. Alexander believes that cultural ideas and values are more important than social class for shaping how people think and act. One of the world's leading social theorists, Alexander outlines his approach to sociology in his book *The Meanings of Social Life* (2003). He has held posts at universities all over the world, including the University of Cambridge in the UK, and has received numerous international awards for his work.

Elijah Anderson (1943–) See pp 26–27

Jean Baudrillard (1929–2007)

The best-known work of French sociologist and philosopher Jean Baudrillard is his examination of the power of the media in society. He found that people's perception of media images today is that they appear more real than the events they are meant to depict, a situation he called "hyperreality." Baudrillard expressed his views in his controversial book *The Gulf War Did Not Take Place* (1991).

Zygmunt Bauman (1925–2017) See pp 132–133

Ulrich Beck (1944–2015) and Elisabeth Beck-Gernsheim (1946–)

German husband-and-wife-team Ulrich Beck and Elisabeth Beck-Gernsheim wrote a number of books together, including *Distant Love* (2013), which is about the changing nature of romantic relationships in a global world. Ulrich Beck believed that globalization increases the risk of environmental disasters and breakdown in social order. He presented these views in his book, *Risk Society* (1992).

Howard Becker (1928–) See pp 84–85

Pierre Bourdieu (1930–2002) See pp 126–127

Samuel Bowles (1939–) and Herbert Gintis (1940–)

While both sociologists are from the US, Samuel Bowles is a Marxist and a professor in economics, and Herbert Gintis is a behavioral scientist and sociobiologist, whose work is guided by the theory that social behavior is influenced by our genes. Together, Bowles and Gintis wrote a classic study about education in a capitalist society, *Schooling in Capitalist America* (1976).

W. E. B. Du Bois (1868–1963)

A US sociologist and civil rights activist, William Du Bois was the first African–American to obtain a doctorate from the University of Harvard, in 1895. After securing a job at the University of Atlanta, he wrote what are now considered classic studies of the identity and experiences of African–American people in US society. The most famous of these are *The Philadelphia Negro* (1899) and *The Souls of Black Folk* (1903). The US Civil Rights Act of 1964, the year after Du Bois died, implemented many of the civil liberties Du Bois had campaigned for all his life, including making racial segregation and discrimination illegal.

Judith Butler (1956–) See pp 20–21

Fernando Henrique Cardoso (1931–)

Brazilian sociologist and politician, Fernando Henrique Cardoso wrote his doctoral thesis at the University of São Paolo on the subject of slavery in Brazil. He has held posts at prestigious universities such as Cambridge, England, Stanford, and the University of California. Always politically active, Cardoso served as the 34th President of Brazil between 1995 and 2003. Now retired from public office, he is committed to putting an end to social problems, and is currently Chair of the Global Commission on Drug Policy.

Manuel Castells (1942–)

Based at the University of Southern California, Manuel Castells is a Spanish sociologist whose work concentrates on globalization and communication. He focuses on the impact of internet-based technologies as the force behind social change. Castells presents his ideas most clearly in *The Rise of the Network Society* (1996).

Nancy Chodorow (1944–)

Feminist sociologist and psychoanalyst Nancy Chodorow spent much of her career at the University of California, Berkeley. She has used her psychoanalytic training as a basis for her sociological work, producing a number of highly influential studies such as *The Reproduction of Mothering: Psychoanalysis and the Sociology of Gender* (1978) and *Feminism and Psychoanalytic Theory* (1989). Now retired, Chodorow continues to lecture around the world.

Patricia Hill Collins (1948–)

Patricia Hill Collins is Distinguished Professor of Sociology at the University of Maryland. She developed the concept of "intersectionality," first coined by Kimberle Crenshaw, which explores the ways in which ethnicity, such as being black, 'intersects" (overlaps) with other aspects of identity such as class and gender. Her book *Black Feminist Thought* (1991) was awarded the C. Wright Mills Award by the American Sociological Association for outstanding and innovative work.

Auguste Comte (1798–1857)

French philosopher Auguste Comte is widely regarded as the founder of sociology. He believed that the methods used in the study of natural sciences, such as biology and chemistry, could also be used to investigate the causes of social problems. Comte thought that modern society should be founded on nonreligious and scientific principles. Comte's views strongly influenced Émile Durkheim (see pp 74–75), the first European university professor of sociology.

Christine Delphy (1941–)
Delphy, a French sociologist and feminist, founded the Women's Liberation Movement in France in 1970. She is a "materialist feminist," meaning that she studies the effect of inequality on women in the domestic environment. She believes that men have exploited women, especially with the marriage contract, which Delphy describes as a "labor contract."

Émile Durkheim (1858–1917) See pp 74–75

Barbara Ehrenreich (1941–)
US feminist Barbara Ehrenreich abandoned an early scientific career to become a writer and political activist. During the 1970s, she held a post at the State University of New York at Old Westbury, where she taught and wrote about the sociology of women's health from a feminist point of view. Ehrenreich's work is much praised and she has received numerous awards. Her bestselling books include *Nickled and Dimed* (2001) and *Living with a Wild God* (2014). She is now a freelance writer and commentator on a wide range of social and political issues.

Norbert Elias (1897–1990)
Norbert Elias was a German thinker forced, as a Jew, to flee his home country when the Nazi Party rose to power before World War II. Elias took refuge in England in 1935. During this time, he continued writing his most famous work *The Civilizing Process* (1939), a historical study of the changes in manners and behavior in Western society from the medieval period onward. The book is now a classic text for sociology students.

Amitai Etzioni (1929–)
An American–Israeli sociologist, Etzioni is best known for his studies of small, self-governing societies. Etzioni believes that the individual members of a community should be granted certain rights and freedoms, providing they contribute to the overall running of their society. He is the author of over 20 books, the most influential of which is *The Active Society*, published in 1968.

Michel Foucault (1926–1984)
Michel Foucault was a philosopher and social theorist. He was especially interested in issues of power and how power is exercised, not only through physical force, but also in the way that people are categorized as different or problematic. In one of his important books, *Discipline and Punish*, published in 1975, he developed his ideas on surveillance. He believed that the effectiveness of surveillance lay in the fact that people only have to think that they are being watched (even though they probably are not) to make them follow the rules. Michel Foucault has been influential not just in sociology, but in many other disciplines too. His ideas have been adopted in the fields of cultural studies, archaeology, and literature, among others.

Harold Garfinkel (1917–2011)
US sociologist Harold Garfinkel was the founder of ethnomethodology: a way of studying society that focuses on how people connect to each other with language, gestures, and behavior. His most famous work, *Studies in Ethnomethodology* (1967), is based on a wide range of firsthand observations. Garfinkel's ideas are now part of mainstream sociology.

Anthony Giddens (1938–) See pp 116–117

Erving Goffman (1922–1982)
The work of Canadian–American sociologist Erving Goffman is most closely associated with the Chicago School of Symbolic Interactionism. This is a school of thought that likens the way we behave socially to a play acted out on stage. In our everyday lives, we perform "roles," which we modify according to what is going on around us. The result is that social life appears predictable and well-directed. For example, we expect a patient in a hospital to act like a sick person. Goffman's work includes *The Presentation of Self in Everyday Life* (1956), *Asylums* (1961), and *Stigma* (1963).

Antonio Gramsci (1891–1937)
The Italian political activist Antonio Gramsci was a Marxist communist. In 1926, he was imprisoned by the Italian Fascist Party, allegedly for being involved in an attempt to murder the Fascist leader, Benito Mussolini. While in prison, Gramsci devised his theory of "cultural hegemony." This refers to the way dominant social groups, the ruling classes, manipulate the values of society to make their own ideas look like "common sense." Any protests, such as saying banks charge too much, are dismissed as "nonsense." Gramsci's ideas, communicated to friends in letters sent from prison, were first published in 1957, 20 years after he died from ill health shortly after being released.

Stuart Hall (1932–2014)
Born in Jamaica, Stuart Hall was one of Britain's most influential sociologists and theorists. His work covered many different areas, but he emphasized the complex experiences of being black and British, and the various ways in which racism operated in British society. Culture was another interest of his, and he led what became known as "The Birmingham School" of research into how young people made sense of their lives by creating subcultures around music and style.

Arlie R. Hochschild (1940–) See pp 64–65

bell hooks (1952–)
African–American feminist Gloria Jean Watkins gave herself the pen name of bell hooks (which she chose to spell with lower case letters). She felt strongly that the feminism of the 1970s and 1980s did not take into account the unique situation of black women or really understand how class made a difference to women's experiences. hooks helped to develop the concept of "intersectionality," which emphasizes that women's oppression is not just gender-based, but must also take account of race and class.

Bruno Latour (1947–)

French philosopher and sociologist Bruno Latour is best known for what is called his "actor-network" theory. His basic idea is that our everyday life is made up of interactions (or networks) between people, and that without such networks, nothing would happen. Bruno claims that networks include technology, which is just as important as people in creating society.

Henri Lefebvre (1901–1991)

French sociologist Henri Lefebvre studied the way cities work and how urban space is defined by control and conflict. In his 1991 book, *The Production of Space*, he outlines how capitalist societies like to treat space as a commercial product, and how ordinary people attempt to resist this. Lefebvre believed that everyone has a "right to the city," which requires a radical approach to take power away from the establishment and social elites.

Michael Löwy (1938–)

Born in Brazil before moving to work in France, Michael Löwy is best known for his writings on Marx and Marxist theory. He champions a romantic critique of capitalism, saying that we need visions of a better future world, built with some of the best aspects of society, such as cooperation, before capitalism took over.

Niklas Luhmann (1927–1998)

German theorist Niklas Luhmann focused on how societies operate. He developed a "systems theory," which says that society is made up of different social systems such as the law, education, the economy, politics, etc. He claimed that each system only really understands wider society in its own terms. For example, the economic system sees everything in terms of money. This causes friction, because the systems clash against each other.

Herbert Marcuse (1898–1979)

German–American Herbert Marcuse was associated with a group of Marxist scholars known as the Frankfurt School. He spent his academic career trying to figure out how consumerism affected people. He claimed that it created false needs (to own a new car, for example) rather than real desires to care for others and to improve the society in which we live.

Karl Marx (1818–1883) See pp 36–37

Helga Nowotny (1937–)

One of Austria's leading sociologists, Helga Nowotny has written extensively on the sociology of science and technology, exploring how society affects science and science affects sociology. She is also interested in the sociology of time and how ideas of time are constructed by different societies in different ways. She discusses this in *Time—The Modern and Postmodern Experience* (1989).

Ann Oakley (1944–)

A prominent British sociologist and feminist, Ann Oakley's work highlights the view that domestic household chores undertaken by women should be regarded as work just as much as paid work that takes place outside the home. In her classic study *The Sociology of Housework* (1974), Oakley argues that housework is one of the many ways that women and their labor are exploited in a male-dominated society. Ann Oakley is also a successful novelist.

George Owusu

The rapid changes in the urban environment of his native Ghana have formed the basis of George Owusu's research. What he reveals is the need to go beyond what Western societies understand about personal space and ownership. African societies need their own models of urban life that, for example, put issues of identity and kinship above economic considerations. George Owusu currently teaches at the University of Ghana.

Ray Pahl (1935–2011)

British sociologist Ray Pahl pointed out that work is not just something people are paid to do in an office or workplace, but also occurs as unpaid arrangements between friends and in the wider community. His breakthrough work was an in-depth study of the working arrangements on the Isle of Sheppey, UK. In the later part of his career, Pahl focused on friendship and the way people maintained connections in a fragmented and challenging world.

Talcott Parsons (1902–1979)

US sociologist Talcott Parsons was associated with a form of sociology we know as structural functionalism. The basic idea of this is that in order to achieve a stable society, everyone must play a part in keeping social order. The key is socialization: learning how to behave in an acceptable way.

Robert D. Putnam (1941–)

US sociologist Robert Putnam is best known for a concept that he called "social capital," which he brought to popular attention in his book *Bowling Alone*, published in 2000. Broadly speaking, he claims that societies work best when people feel and maintain close bonds of community. Putnam believes that the more ties people have with others, the better the chances of societies enjoying good health, low levels of crime, and all-around happiness.

Alberto Guerreio Ramos (1915–1982)

Guerrio Ramos was a strong critic of the way that sociological studies in his native Brazil did nothing to improve the lives of the minority groups living there. The lack of solutions to the problems many people faced inspired his thoughts on what makes a good society. He saw that society was too complicated to be seen in terms of one thing, such as production or consumption of goods, or the availability of money.

Adrienne Rich (1929–2012)

US academic Adrienne Rich was a feminist poet and essayist. Her work examines how gay and lesbian people are sidelined and stigmatized in society. Rich thought that the idea of heterosexuality is forced upon us, either directly through what people say, or indirectly through the way sexuality is portrayed in popular culture such as books, films, and newspapers.

George Ritzer (1940–)

US sociologist George Ritzer argues that many aspects of everyday life are increasingly being organized like a fast-food burger chain. By this he means that everything is becoming the same and we get exactly what we expect. This makes life dull, because there are no surprises, and any sense of excitement or something different happening is lost.

Hartmut Rosa (1965–)

Rosa's work draws on fellow German Karl Marx's ideas of alienation, the feeling of being distanced from life because we have no control over it. He argues that modern society now moves so fast that people struggle, in what seems like less and less time, to keep up with all the demands made of them. The result is a sense of not being able to find our true selves and do the things we want to.

Edward Said (1935–2003)

A Palestinian–American, Edward Said explored the experiences of peoples who were colonized by Europe and America. His key text, *Orientalism*, was published in 1978 and dealt with how Western culture misrepresented people in the East as being somehow feeble and inferior.

Saskia Sassen (1949–) See pp 112–113

Andrew Sayer (1949–)

British sociologist Andrew Sayer's best-known work is *The Moral Significance of Class* (2005), which considers ethical and moral issues in relation to inequality. Sayer is interested in the ways class shapes how people think about and value themelves and others, as well as the relationship between social class and morality.

Richard Sennett (1943–)

Writing on a wide range of topics, US sociologist Richard Sennett has explored what he sees as the damaging effects of capitalism on the lives of ordinary people. One of his most important claims is that capitalism has drained life of meaning. Sennett thinks this is especially true in the workplace, where modern management styles prevent employees from gaining job satisfaction and a sense of their own worth.

Georg Simmel (1858–1918)

German sociologist Georg Simmel based his work on small-scale observations of everyday life: how people walked and talked and moved around the city. He was fascinated to see how urban living shaped people's awareness of their surroundings. Simmel's work laid the foundations for urban sociology and studies of the ways in which people communicate and interact.

Boaventura de Sousa Santos (1940–) See pp 106–107

Ferdinand Tönnies (1855–1936)

One of the world's first sociologists, the German Ferdinand Tönnies tried to understand the fast-moving and dramatic changes he witnessed in the society of his day. What especially interested him was how the expansion of urban life was altering the traditional bonds people had with each other. He identified the tension between the *Gemeinschaft* (community) of rural life with the *Gessellschaft* (association) of urban life.

Bryan S. Turner (1945–)

Born in England, Turner has lived all over the world, and has taught in universities in Europe, Asia, the United States, and Australia. The sociological topics he has tackled cover everything from how we think about our bodies, from a cultural as well as a biological point of view, to the way in which religions have been transformed by modern society.

Thorstein Veblen (1857–1929)

A Norwegian–American, Thorstein Veblen was one of the first sociologists to try and understand what we call consumer culture: a society in which our values and lifestyles are shaped by the purchase and use of goods and services. He noted how people tried to imitate the consumer habits of the wealthier members of society as a way of raising their own social status, for which he coined the expression "conspicuous consumption." The term "Veblen goods" is used to describe goods for which demand increases the more expensive they become.

Löic Wacquant (1960–)

The increase in the numbers of people being imprisoned has been at the center of Löic Wacquant's work, both in his home country of France and in the US. He argues that crowded jails actually have nothing to do with rising crime. Instead, Wacquant believes that imprisonment is being used as a way of oppressing certain ethnic minority groups and people on the margins of society.

Sylvia Walby (1953–)

Prominent British feminist sociologist Sylvia Walby has done much research into the effects of patriarchy (male power) in society. She identified patriarchy in six spheres of life: in culture, the workplace, politics, sexuality, the law, and in violence against women. Walby has worked for UNESCO in developing policies to promote gender equality on a global level.

Max Weber (1864–1920) See pp 58–59

Charles Wright Mills (1916–1962) See pp 46–47

Sharon Zukin

The city has long been an area of study for sociologists. US academic Sharon Zukin's work has shed light on the processes behind "gentrification": the reworking of districts to meet higher-class standards. Her study, *Loft Living* (1982), discusses how the SoHo area of New York, once a district of garment manufacturers and later artist studios, became a more desirable neighborhood of upscale apartments and boutiques. Her 2010 book, *Naked City*, also focuses on New York, and how gentrification has robbed the city of its soul.

Glossary

Activist
A person with strong political or social beliefs who takes action to change an existing system. Activists usually belong to organized groups.

Agency
In sociology, a person's ability to act independently and make free choices.

Alienation
A term used in **Marxism** to mean a feeling of disconnect from friends, job, and society. Alienation is common among workers who have no say in what they do or which goods they produce.

Anomie
A state of aimlessness and confusion. It is what people experience when "normal" society suddenly breaks down and familiar rules and standards no longer have any meaning.

Blue-collar worker
A description of a person who works in manual labor rather than has a "desk" job. The term refers to the blue shirts commonly worn by laborers in the early 20th century. (See also **White-collar worker.**)

Business class
The people who own and run businesses, using paid employees to do the work.

Capitalism
A type of economic system in which businesses and services can be privately owned and run for profit by individuals, rather than by a government.

Class
A group of people who are broadly equal in terms of power, wealth, and social status.

Climate change
Long-term change in global temperatures and weather patterns. Most scientists agree that human activity, such as the burning of fossil fuels, is contributing to the current warming of the world's climate.

Colonialism
A system in which one country takes over another and turns it into a settled colony. The parent nation, which holds all the political power, exploits the resources of the colony for financial profit.

Community
A group of people who have an interest or a characteristic in common. They may not live in the same place.

Conspicuous consumption
Spending money on expensive and unnecessary goods and services for the purpose of displaying wealth and status.

Consumer
A person who buys goods and services for his or her own use.

Cooperative
A business that is owned and run by its workers. The members of a cooperative all have a say in decision-making and a share in the profits.

Cultural omnivore
Someone who enjoys various social activities, from "highbrow" culture, such as ballet, to "popular" culture, such as rock music.

Culture
The arts, activities, ideas, customs, and values shared by members of a particular group or society.

Data
Statistics, numbers, and other items of information collected for study, analysis, or reference.

Data set
A collection of pieces of information for computer processing—for example, census data—which may be looked at as separate items or as a set.

Dataveillance
Tracking of people's activities through their personal electronic data systems. Includes monitoring a person's mobile phone calls, internet usage, and emails.

Depression
A long-term mental disorder that causes feelings of sadness, hopelessness, and lack of interest in life. People with depression may also experience physical problems, commonly including headaches, joint pains, and extreme fatigue.

Deviant
A person or a type of behavior that breaks the normal rules of a particular society.

Dialectic
Two opposing points of view that come together to create something new.

Discrimination
The unfair treatment of people because of such characteristics as their skin color, sex, and age.

Domestic work
Unpaid work in the home, such as cooking, cleaning, and childcare.

Elite
A group of people who have the highest standing in society, together with the greatest wealth and the most power.

Emotional labor
Work that requires employees to manage their feelings as part of the job. For example, to boost a company's image, a person might be asked to always appear friendly or sympathetic toward members of the public.

Employment
The state of being in paid work.

Environment
The surroundings in which a person, animal, or plant lives.

Environmental racism
Ignoring the environmental rights of minority groups by, for example, exposing people to hazardous chemicals or destroying their natural homelands.

Ethnicity
The language, culture, and beliefs that give a group its **identity**.

Ethnography
The scientific study of people and their cultures.

Feminism
The belief that women and men should have equal social, political, and financial rights.

Focus group
A research method often used by sociologists, involving a group of people who come together to talk about a special issue or situation.

Gemeinshaft
A German word meaning "community." The term describes deep bonds and shared values between people.

Gender
The social and cultural beliefs about men and women, as well as their biological differences.

Gesellschaft
A German word meaning "association." The term describes the practical, functional, and nonpersonal relationships between people in a larger organization or area.

Globalization
The process by which societies around the world connect with each other through trade, industry, communications, and cultural exchanges.

Glocalization
The mixing of values when globally available consumer goods and services are adapted to suit local tastes and cultures.

Habitus
The lifestyle and cultural tastes shared by people who belong to a particular social group.

Hegemony
The power or authority that one group uses to control others.

Heterosexual
A person who is attracted to people of the opposite sex.

Identity
The sense of who we are, and how other people see us in terms of such characteristics as **gender**, appearance, and personality.

Individualism
The idea that each person's freedom to think and act is the most important thing in a society.

Institutions
The rules of organizations that form the building blocks of society, such as religion, education, and the law.

Marxism

A social theory developed from the ideas of the 19th-century German thinkers and sociologists Karl Marx (see pp.36–37) and Friedrich Engels. Marxism says there are two main classes in society. One, the ruling class, exploits the other, the working class, for its own profit. Marx believed this unfair system must be overthrown.

Mass society

A modern industrialized society mostly made up of groups of people that share a general culture, but who are not closely connected to each other.

Media

Sometimes known as mass media, the various types of communication that bring information to the public. These include newspapers, radio, television, and the internet.

Mental illness

One of a wide range of conditions that can affect a person's mood, feelings, personality, and behavior to varying degrees.

Middle class

A social group between the **elite** and the **working class**. Middle-class people tend to be **white-collar workers** with relatively secure lifestyles, and intermediate levels of wealth.

Moral duty

The responsibility people have to act in ways that society thinks is right.

Norm

A generally accepted social rule or standard.

Poverty

Lack of basic needs, such as food, housing, and clothing, is called absolute poverty. Relative poverty means lack of the minimum amount of possessions or income acceptable within a society.

Precariat

Term combining the words "precarious" (insecure) with "proletariat" (working people) to describe people without job security or reliable income.

Proletariat

A Marxist term describing **working-class** people.

Racism

Unjust treatment of a group of people because of their ethnic origins and skin color. Racism is based on assumptions about supposed biological differences.

Rationalization

The theory of German economist and sociologist Max Weber (see pp.58–59) that modern society is increasingly organized around the values of reason, logic, and efficiency.

Rehabilitation

Restoring to normality. The goal of rehabilitating criminal offenders, commonly through therapy or education, is to help them integrate back into society.

Religion

A system of belief in a god or gods, or other supernatural power. Most religions involve rites and ceremonies of some kind.

Roles

The types of behavior expected of people in society, often related to their **gender** or age.

Rural

Relating to the countryside.

Secularization

The change that occurs when religion loses its influence and other cultural values and rules become more important to society.

Semi-structured interview

A sociological research method that engages the interviewee in an informal conversation and encourages free expression.

Sexism

Prejudice against and unfair treatment of people because of their biological sex.

Social class

One of the social groups into which people are often placed according to such factors as their wealth, education, and status. (See **Elite; Middle class; Working class.**)

Social construction

An idea that is shaped by a person's social background rather than based in reality. For example, beliefs about **class**, **gender**, sexuality, or race are often social constructions.

Socialization
The process by which people, especially children, learn to fit into society and behave as expected.

Social media
Websites and phone apps that allow users to communicate online, sharing information, news, and ideas, and making friendships.

Social mobility
The movement of people, either as individuals or groups, from one **social class** to another.

Social structure
The social **institutions** and relationships that make up the framework of a society.

State
A general term for a nation or political region with recognized borders and an organized system of government. A state can also be a distinct area within a nation, as in the US.

Status
A person's social and professional standing within a society.

Stereotype
A widespread and firmly fixed assumption about the characteristics of a person or group of people. Stereotyping often gives such a simplified view that it creates an exaggerated or inaccurate image.

Structure
Part of a person's life, such as **social class** or ethnic origin, that is beyond any individual's control.

Stigma
A strong sense of disgrace or public disapproval that prevents a person from being fully accepted in a society.

Subculture/Subtribe
A group of people whose shared interests and behaviors set them apart from mainstream society. Subcultures often identify themselves by wearing distinctive clothes, listening to certain types of music, or giving themselves a collective name.

Surveillance
Close observation of people and places to prevent crime. Surveillance may involve technologies such as CCTV cameras and **dataveillance,** which uses computer software to monitor someone's personal data.

Survey
Often used in sociological research, an information-gathering method consisting of a series of carefully designed questions. Surveys aim to find out as much as possible about what people do and think.

Transgender
A term that describes a person whose behavior and sense of identity does not align with his or her biological sex. (*See also* **Transsexual**)

Transnational corporation (TNC)
A large business enterprise comprising a parent company and a network of related companies that operate in many countries round the world. TNCs are sometimes also referred to as multinational corporations.

Transsexual
Someone who has a strong desire to become a member of the opposite sex. A transsexual person may seek medical and surgical help to achieve a change of physical appearance. (*See also* **Transgender.**)

Urban
Relating to a town or city.

Values
What people in a society believe to be the right behavior, aims, and attitudes.

Virtual identity
A personal profile created online for **social media**, which may not be an accurate picture of the user.

White-collar worker
Someone whose job does not involve manual labor, such as an office worker. (*See also* **Blue-collar worker.**)

Work ethic
A belief in the value of hard work, which is said to improve a person's worth and character.

Working class
The traditional description of people who do a variety of skilled or unskilled jobs, but generally have low social status. (*See also* **Blue-collar worker.**)

Index

Note: **bold** page numbers are used to indicate key information on the topic.

A

absolute poverty 98
abuse 25, 32
academic sociologists 8–9
acid rain 119
advertising 122, 137
African-Americans *see* black people
afterlife 51
age, and identity 30–31
agency 100
agnosticism 53
air travel, low-cost 110, 118, 131
Al-Akhawayn Bukhari 90
Alexander, Jeffrey **148**
alienation 26, 37, 61, 68, 90
Anderson, Elijah **26–7**
anomie 74, 90
anxiety 88, 89, 131
Ariès, Phillipe 38
ARPANET 146
Arrighi, Giovanni 105
automation 62, 63, 66

B

Ball, Kirstie 66
Baudrillard, Jean **148**
Bauman, Zygmunt 7, 108–9, 130–31, **132–3**
Beauvoir, Simone de 38
Beck, Ulrich 119, **148**
Beck-Gernsheim, Elisabeth **148**

Becker, Howard **84–5**
benefits, state 99
Bentham, Jeremy 81
Berger, Peter 44
biology, and gender identity 16
black people 25, 26–7, 38, 39, 87, 91, 102–3
blended families 33
blue-collar workers 35
body, and identity 15
Bourdieu, Pierre 35, 43, 101, 124–5, **126–7**
Bowles, Samuel 42–3, **148**
boys 16–17
Braverman, Harry 66
Broken Windows Theory 91
Buddhism 50, 52
Bull, Michael 141
Busfield, Joan 88
business 45
    and media 137
    and power 48
    sociologists in 8–9
    and white-collar crime 78–9
business class 96–7
Butler, Judith 17, **20–21**

C

Campbell, Colin 122
capitalism 36, 37, 102, 108
    religion and 51, 58–9, 61
Cardoso, Fernando Henrique **148**
Castells, Manuel 109, 140, 142, **148**
CCTV 66, 67, 80–81, 91
celebrity culture 119
Chan, Angelique 30
Charkalis, Roy 143

Chicago School 54
childhood 38
children
    abuse of 32
    and family experience 32
China 105
Chodorow, Nancy **148**
Chomsky, Noam 136–7, 144
Christianity 51, 52–3, 103
church attendance 50, 52–3
cities 54–5, 68, 69, 113
    global 112
citizen journalists 137
civil partnerships 33
civil rights 25
Clarke, Roger 66
class 34–5, 46
    and culture 124, 125, 126
    and education 43
    and identity 14, 34–5, 38, 116
    Marx on 36–7, 38
    social mobility 101
climate change 114, 117
cognitive justice 107
Collins, Patricia Hill **148**
colonialism 102, 104, 118
color choice
    and gender 16
    and subcultures 23
"Comic-con" events 22
The Communist Manifesto (Marx/Engels) 36, 37
community
    and environment 115
    ethnography 11
    and religion 51, 75
    sense of 56–7, 68, 69, 122
    urban and rural 54–5, 68
community service 76
Comte, Auguste **148–9**
conformity 43
connectivity 110, 142, 143

Connell, Raewyn 17
conspicuous consumption 96–7
consumer goods 35, 89, 96–7, 110, 122–3, 124, 127, 131, 133, 142, 146
control 62, 81
    individual vs society 100
core nations 104–5
correspondence theory 43
crime
    breaking rules 76–7
    deviant behavior 84–5
    motivation for 72–3
    solving 82–3
    white-collar 78–9
cultural capital 35, 43, 127
cultural imperialism 110
cultural omnivores 124
culture 45, 124–5, 126–7, 131, 146
curriculum 42–3
cyberbullying 145

D

data sets 11
dataveillance 66–7
Davis, Kingsley 100
Delphy, Christine **149**
depression 88, 89
developing countries 104–5
deviants 84–5, 90
digital exclusion 144
DiMaggio, Paul 143
disadvantaged groups 72, 100, 101, 113
disapproval, fear of 77
discrimination
    against developing countries 104
    against homosexuals 29

against mentally ill 89
against women 16, 18
racial 24, 25
disenchantment 58, 59, 64, 74
divorce 32, 130
domestic work 19, 48, 60
Douglas, John 83
dress
and class 35
and identity 14, 122–3
and subcultures 23
Du Bois, W. E. B. 38, 43, 102, **148**
Durkheim, Émile 35, 50, 51, 52, 68, 72, **74–5**, 76, 77, 90

E

economic capital 35, 127
economics, developing countries 104–5
ecosystems 109, 119
education 42–3, 45, 69, 101, 127
Ehrenreich, Barbara 95, **149**
Eitzen, D. Stanley 79
Elias, Norbert 77, **149**
elite 45, 46, 48, 61
Ellis, Vaughan 62
emotions 64, 65
employment see work
Engels, Friedrich 36, 37
Enlightenment 29, 52
environmental problems 107, 108, 109, 114–15, 117, 119, 123, 131
equality see inequality
ethnicity 14, 24, 83
and health 87
ethnography 11
Etzioni, Amitai **149**

F

Facebook 25, 67, 95, 109, 140, 144, 145, 147
Fair Trade 109, 119
fake news 147
family 32–3, 45
fear 77, 131, 137
femininity 17, 20, 21
feminism 7, 18
focus groups 10
Foucault, Michel 29, 48–9, 81, 91, **149**
functionalism 74

G

gangs 85
Gans, Herbet 135
Garfinkel, Harold **149**
Garland, David 76, 77
gatekeepers, media 138–9
Gay Rights movement 29, 39
Gemeinschaft 54, 55
gender identity 14, 16–21, 38
Gesellschaft 54, 55
the ghetto 27
Giddens, Anthony 15, 108, 110, 114, **116–17**
Gilroy, Paul 103
Gintis, Herbert 42–3, **148**
girls 16–17
glass ceiling 18
global equality 107
global warming 114, 117
globalization 35, 93, 106, 107, 108–9, 110, 112–13, 118, 131
glocalization 110–11
Gobineau, Arthur de 103
Goffman, Erving 15, 44, 89, **149**

Goths 22, 23
government 45, 65, 137
Gramsci, Antonio **149**
greenhouse gases 114, 115
Grint, Keith 60

H I

habitus 124, 125, 126, 127
Hall, Stuart 39, **149**
health 86–9, 90
and community 57
and equality 86–7
and hegemonic masculinity 17
mental illness 88–9
and racial discrimination 25, 87
hegemonic masculinity 17
heteronormativity 29
Higgs, Paul 30–31
Hindman, Matthew 141
Hochschild, Arlie **64–5**
Holocaust 20, 132
homophobia 7, 29
homosexuality 15, 21, 29, 90
hooks, bell 39, **149**
Howker, Ed 31
human rights 20, 103, 106
identity 14–15, 116, 144
and age 30–31, 39
and class 34–5, 38, 116
and consumerism 122–3, 133
and cultural tastes 124, 125, 126, 131
factors creating 14–15
and family 32–3, 38
and gender 16–21, 38
intersectionality 39
and leisure activities 129
and race 24–7, 38

and sexuality 28–9, 39
and subcultures 22–3, 39
and work 14, 60, 62, 122, 130
immigration 113
individualism 57, 59, 86
Industrial Revolution 6, 54, 66, 96
inequality 6
developing countries 104–5
divided world 106
and globalization 107
and health 30, 86–7
and institutions 45
and mental illness 88–9
of opportunity 100–101
and poverty trap 98–9
and race 24, 25, 38, 102–3
and status 96–7
and superrich 94–5
and women 18–19, 65
Information Age 140–41
institutional racism 25
institutionalization 44
institutions 40–69, 75
internet 130, 134, 140, 142–3 143, 145, 146, 147
intersectionality 39
interviews, "semi-structured" 10
isolation 89, 142, 143

J K L

James, Oliver 89
Jefferson, Tony 39
Jenkins, Richard 14, 122
jobs see work
Judaism 20, 53, 75, 132
Kan, Man Yee 19
Das Kapital (Marx) 36, 37
Kelling, George 91

knowledge 106, 107
    and media 136, 141
labeling theory 84–5
labor 36, 64, 65
language 23, 35
Latour, Bruno **150**
law 45, 49, 76–7, 82–3
Lefebvre, Henri 54, **150**
leisure class 96, 128
leisure time 128–9
lesbians 29, 39
life expectancy 30, 86, 87
Link, Bruce 89
liquid modernity 130–31,
    133
Livingstone, Sonia 145
Löwy, Michael **150**
Luckmann, Thomas 44
Luhmann, Niklas **150**
Lupton, Deborah 143
Luther, Martin 51
Lynd, Robert and Helen 56

M N
McLuhan, Marshall 146
McMillan, Sally 144
Madison, James 141
Malik, Shiv 31
Marcuse, Herbert **150**
marginalization 38, 39, 72,
    143
marriage 32, 33, 45, 130
Martinez, Joseph 79
Marx, Karl/Marxism 6, 7, 34,
    36–7, 38, 48, 50, 51, 52, 53,
    61, 68
masculinity 17, 20, 21
mass media 134–5
media
    bias 134, 139
    influence of 134–5
    new media sources 141

news selection 138–9
    ownership of 136–7
medicalization 91
mental illness 15, 88–9, 90,
    131
Merton, Robert 72
methodological
    individualism 59
middle class 34–5, 46, 101,
    125
Moore, Wilbert 100
moral standards 72, 77, 135
Murray, Charles 99
music, and subcultures 22,
    23
natural resources 114–15
new managerialism 62
news 134, 135, 136
    interpretation of 134, 135
    media sources 140–41
    reliability of 136, 141, 147
    selection of stories 138–9
    newspapers 135, 136, 138,
        140, 147
norms 22, 29, 32, 43, 44
Nowotny, Helga **150**

O P
Oakley, Ann 19, **150**
O'Brien, Rosaleen 17
old age 30–31, 39
online presence 144–5
opportunism 83
opportunities, equal
    100–101, 117
Orwell, George 80–81
outsiders 85
Owusu, George **150**
Pahl, Ray 56, **150**
Pakulski, Jan 35
Panopticon 81
Park, Robert E. 54

Parsons, Talcott 32, 90, **150**
pay gap, gender 18, 19
peripheral nations 104–5
persecution 113, 132
Peterson, Richard 124, 138
Phelan, Jo 89
Pickerill, Jenny 115
Pickett, Kate 88
Piketty, Thomas 95
police 8, 77, 91
    and racism 25
political elite 35
politics 9, 65, 117, 137
poverty 55, 69, 100, 112
    and health 87
    poverty trap 98–9
power 48–9, 81, 84, 97, 105
precariat 63, 69
prison 15, 44, 77, 81
privacy 67, 144, 145
profiling, criminal 82–3
punishment 43, 76–7
Putnam, Robert D. **150**

Q R
Queer Theory 21
race, and identity 14, 24–7,
    38
racial tension 91
racialization 24
racism 7, 25, 26–7
    development of 102–3
    environmental 115
Ramos, Alberto Guerreiro
    150
rationalization 59
recycling 115
regional identity 122
rehabilitation 76, 77
relative poverty 98
religion 14, 45, 50–53, 68,
    75, 116, 122

renewable energy 115
research methods 10–11
resistance, to power 49
responsibility, individual vs
    society 100–101
Rich, Adrienne **150**
risk 86, 133
Ritzer, George **151**
Robertson, Roland 105,
    110–11
Rojek, Chris 119, 128–9
Rosa, Hartmut **151**
Roseto Effect 57
rules, breaking 76–7
ruling class 35, 36
rural life 54–5

S
Said, Edward **151**
same-sex relationships 29,
    33, 90
Sassen, Saskia **112–13**
Sayer, Andrew 95, **151**
schools 42–3, 101
Schudson, Michael 138
science, and religion 52
Scott, Susie 91
sea levels 115, 117
secularization 52, 53
security, job 62, 69
segregation, racial 24
self-identity 116, 122–3
selfies 14, 15, 144
semi-peripheral nations
    104–5
Sennett, Richard 62, **151**
serial offenders 82, 83
sexuality
    and identity 14, 28–9, 39
    Queer Theory 21
    and society 28–9
shopping 122–3, 129, 133

Silva, Jennifer 31
Simmel, Georg **151**
single-parent families 33
slavery 102–3
slums 55, 69, 106
social capital 35, 43, 57, 101, 127
social change 131, 142
social cohesion 50
social constructs 14–15
  childhood 38
  gender 17, 21
  news 138, 139
  race 24
social facts 75
social justice 117, 126
social media 15, 67, 109, 140, 143, 144, 145, 147
social networking 43, 131, 142, 144, 145, 147
social position 101
social pressure 72
social structures 100
socialization
  and family 32
  gender 16–17
society
  fairer 117
  foundations of 44–5
  responsibilities of 100–101
  role of the family in 32–3
  structure of 44, 74
sociologists 6, 7
  research methods 10–11
  role of 8–9
Sousa Santos, Boaventura de **106–7**
space of flows 109
space, and power 48–9
Stahl, Garth 43
standard of living 31, 108
Standing, Guy 63, 69
status 34, 35, 83
  gaining 96

and health 87
loss of 97
and wealth 96–7
and work 60–61
stepparent families 33
stereotypes
  family 32
  gender 19
  mental health 88
  old age 31
  racial 87
stigmatization 15, 25, 89
Strain Theory 72
street-corner life 26
subcultures 22–3, 39
superrich 94–5
surveillance 66–7, 80–81, 91
surveys 11
Sutherland, Edwin 78
Sutton, Philip 115

T U

Taylor, Phil 62
television 135, 136, 138, 139, 140, 146, 147
Third Way 117
Thorpe, Holly 129
Tönnies, Ferdinand 54, **151**
tourism 119
trade unions 48
transnational corporations (TNCs) 108–9, 110, 131
tribes 22–3, 39
trolling 145
Tulle, Emmanuelle 30
Turner, Bryan S. 53, **151**
"Unabomber" (Theodore Kaczynski) 83
uncertainty 51, 81, 130–31, 133
unemployment 99
urban life 54–5, 68, 69, 81

V W

values
  and community 54, 55, 56, 76
  and culture 124, 130
  family 32
  and institutions 44
  and religion 50, 122
  subcultures 23
Veblen, Thorstein 95, 96, 97, **151**
violence
  in the family 32
  and street codes 26
virtual communities 56, 131, 142, 143
virtual identity 144, 145
Wacquant, Löic 95, **151**
wages
  minimum 95
  stagnation of 101
  women's 18
Walby, Sylvia 48, **151**
Wallerstein, Immanuel 104–5, 108
war
  and migration 113, 131
waste disposal 114–15
Waters, Malcolm 35
wealth
  distribution of 35
  and status 96–7
  and superrich 94–5
Weber, Max 35, 46, 50, 51, 52, **58–9**, 61, 68, 97
websites
  file-sharing 137
  news 138
  reliability of 143
welfare benefits 99
white-collar crime 78–9
white-collar workers 35, 46
Wilkinson, Richard 88

Willmott, Peter 55
Wilson, James 91
Wirth, Louis 54
Wollstonecraft, Mary 38
women
  abuse of 32, 48
  gender identity 16, 38
  leisure time 129
  men's power over 48
  and work 18–19, 45, 64, 65
work 60–63, 69
  and education 42–3
  and identity 14, 60, 62, 122, 130
  low-paid 95, 99
  micromanagement 62–3
  power of employment 48, 61
  women 18–19, 45, 64, 65
  workplace technology 66–7
work ethic, Protestant 51, 59, 61, 68
working class 34–5, 36, 43, 65, 101
world system 104–5
Wright Mills, Charles 7, **46–7**

Y Z

Young, Iris Marion 17
Young, Michael 55
youth
  cult of 30
  living online 144, 145
  problems of 31, 62, 63
  and subcultures 22–3, 39
zero-tolerance 91
Zuckerberg, Mark 94–5, 147
Zukin, Sharon **151**

Acknowledgments

Dorling Kindersley would like to thank Dr. Megan Todd for writing the Introduction (pp6–7); Hazel Beynon for editing the biographies and proofreading; and Helen Peters for the index.

The publisher would like to thank the following for their kind permission to reproduce their photographs:

(Key: a–above; b–below/bottom; c–center; f–far; l–left; r–right; t–top)

6 Alamy Stock Photo: Image Source (c). Dreamstime.com: Darrinhenry (cl); Syda Productions (cr). 6-7 123RF.com: Igor Zakharevich (c). 7 Alamy Stock Photo: Phanuwat Nandee (tr); NASA Archive (tl). Dreamstime.com: Ian Allenden (cr); Pawel Szczepanski (c). 17 Dreamstime.com: Atholpady (ca). 18 Getty Images: Historical (cb). 23 Dreamstime.com: Kristina Afanasyeva (tr). 25 Dreamstime.com: Yanik Chauvin (br). 29 Dreamstime.com: Olga Besnard (br). 30 Getty Images: David Madison (bc). 32 Getty Images: Vstock LLC (bc). 35 Getty Images: Monty Rakusen (bc). 44 Dreamstime.com: Tyler Olson (bc). 49 Getty Images: AFP (br). 51 Getty Images: Daily Herald Archive / SSPL (br). 53 Alamy Stock Photo: Roger Parkes (cra). 54 123RF.com: William Perugini (bc). 57 Dreamstime.com: Milla74 (br). 61 Alamy Stock Photo: OJO Images Ltd (br). 63 University of Birmingham: STRANDS - strands-project.eu (br). 66 123RF.com: Ximagination (cb). Dreamstime.com: Mystock88photo (cb). 79 123RF.com: feverpitched (bl). 83 Getty Images: Boston Globe (tr). 89 Alamy Stock Photo: Lumi Images (bc). 92-93 Dreamstime.com: Paura. 95 Alamy Stock Photo: Martin Thomas Photography (crb). 97 Getty Images: Image Source RF / Cadalpe (cra). 99 Getty Images: JGI / Jamie Grill (ca). 101 Dreamstime.com: Chicco7 (tr). 105 Dreamstime.com: Dibrova (cra). 109 Dreamstime.com: Buccaneer (br). 111 123RF.com: Serghei Starus (br). 115 Dreamstime.com: Savone (bc). 120-121 Dreamstime.com: Hongqi Zhang (aka Michael Zhang). 122 Dreamstime.com: Ciolca (bc). 124 Alamy Stock Photo: Peter Jordan_NE (bc). 129 Dreamstime.com: Alan Dyck (br). 131 Getty Images: Maciej Noskowski (ca). 135 123RF.com: Tatiana Gladskikh (br). 141 123RF.com: Daniel Jędzura (tr). 145 123RF.com: Cathy Yeulet (cra).

All other images © Dorling Kindersley
For further information see: www.dkimages.com